Sons & Daughters
EMERGING

A Prayer Strategy *for*
Millennial Parents

Sons &
Daughters

E M E R G I N G

LISA Z. BLADY

Carpenter's Son Publishing

Published by Carpenter's Son Publishing, Franklin, Tennessee

NIV, NLT, ESV, BSB (Berean Study Bible), MSG (Message Translation), PST (Passion Translation), NASB, KJB, CSB, God's Word Translation, New American Standard 1977, Jubilee Bible 2000, King James 2000 Bible, American King James Version, American Standard Version, Young's Literal Translation

Edited by Adept Content Solutions

Cover Design by Nelly Sanchez

Interior Design by Adept Content Solutions

Printed in the United States of America

978-1-949572-55-1

This book is dedicated to my grandchildren:

Twin baby boys now in heaven (6/14/13)

Lennon Harper Theriot (7/7/15)

Remi Everly Theriot (12/19/16)

Hayes Anna-Lynn Theriot (4/18/18)

and

Diana Theresa Melancon-Zeringue (9/19/39–12/8/17),

aka "Momma" or "Maw Maw" (without whom

none of this would have been possible)

CONTENTS

INTRODUCTION

"A person's a person, no matter how small."

Congratulations! As you start this journey of life with your baby, you may still be in disbelief and shock. That is okay! Each life, each pregnancy, is different. We are going to walk together as we pray over your baby as they develop and grow!

I remember the day I found out I was pregnant with my son; I stood there in shock, not believing that "it" had actually happened. I soon scheduled my appointment with the doctor, and the whole examination went very clinical, until she popped her head back into the room and said "Oh, I almost forgot, we need to listen for the heartbeat!" It was my first pregnancy, and I didn't know what to expect. Then she placed the fetal Doppler on my belly, and I heard his heart beat for the very first time. Everything inside me crumbled, and without warning, I broke down and cried. For weeks, my head knew I was pregnant, but for the first time, my heart was now connected with this little human being who was growing inside my belly. That was twenty-eight years ago, and today that little boy is now married and a father with three beautiful and perfect little girls of his own.

Those three little girls are the reason I decided to write this prayer journal. When my daughter-in-law was pregnant with her first child, I was walking through my home, minding my own business when Holy Spirit asked me, "Lisa, why aren't you praying for this baby?" It was one of those moments where I was stopped dead in my tracks because the only answer I could respond with was a stutter. Immediately, I remembered that verse from the Bible that everyone recites when they talk about pregnancy.

> For you created my inmost being;
> you knit me together in my mother's womb.
> I praise you because I am fearfully and wonderfully made;
> your works are wonderful,
> I know that full well.
> My frame was not hidden from you
> when I was made in the secret place,
> when I was woven together in the depths of the earth.
> Your eyes saw my unformed body;
> all the days ordained for me were written in your book
> before one of them came to be.

—Psalm 139:13-16 NIV

"He knit me together in my mother's womb." My daughter-in-law was twenty weeks pregnant at the time, and for the first time those verses leaped off the page and made sense. I was unfamiliar of what was developing at that particular week but stood there amazed thinking, *Wow! This week He could be creating the brain, next week the eyelashes and the next week He could be building her lungs.* The whole process became very real for me in that moment. So, like any good

millennial grandmother, I began tracking each week and praying as each organ made its entrance into her little body.

Enter Lennon Harper. On July 7, a perfect day for a perfect little girl, I remember holding her for the first time and staring at every inch in amazement, partly because she was my first grandchild, but also because I'd prayed for her every step of the way. I was amazed with her legs and how her thighs were so tiny and, as silly as it sounds, I marveled at her knee caps—in awe of the complexity of everything that went into that one little part of her body. I just kept whispering to God, "You didn't miss a thing! How do you do it? How does all of this come from one cell?"

Just nine months later, on Mother's Day I got another surprise that Remi Everly would soon be on the scene. Here comes baby number 2! I'd realized that so many of us just wait for that appointed day of arrival and leave everything up to chance that a healthy baby will be delivered at the end of the term—and typically there is! But why do we leave things up to chance? The pregnancy went well, and in December of that same year we had ourselves another beautiful little girl to add to our family. Only this time, God impressed upon me to write a book about how to pray during a pregnancy. As time went on, the pieces of the puzzle came together, and the idea still seemed much more like mine than God's, until the turning of the New Year. While a couple was praying over me, the wife asked if I write—that she felt God was telling me that this is the season to write that book! I was blown away by how specific it was because she had no idea I'd been working on it for six months.

Eight months later, I was given the news that we were going to have yet *another* addition to our family. Hayes Anna-Lynn reminded everyone on the outside with her constant kicks inside her mother's belly that she was soon going to give her big sister Lennon a run for her money.

As the book began to take shape, the turning of yet another year came upon me, and a different lady prayed over me at the same Christian luncheon as the previous year in Destin, Florida, called Business Empowered. Again, the prayer came out that the "writer anointing in me was coming forth, loud, stirred up, fired, and quickened!"

So here we are—you and I—birthing something new. I pray that as *you pray* these next nine months, you will recognize God's voice and heart for you and your baby.

A Foundation for Weeks Ahead

Before we venture any further, I want to look at Psalm 139 in the New Living Translation to help us lay the foundation for weeks ahead.

> *You* made all the delicate, inner parts of my body
> and *knit me together in my mother's womb.*
> *Thank you for making me* so wonderfully complex!
> Your workmanship is marvelous—how well I know it.
> *You watched me as I was being formed in utter seclusion,*
> as I was woven together in the dark of the womb.
> You saw me before I was born.
> Every day of my life was recorded in your book.
> *Every moment was laid out*
> *before a single day had passed.*

Did you read only what was italicized?

> *You*
> *knit me together in my mother's womb.*
> *Thank you for making me*
> *You watched me as I was being formed in utter seclusion,*
> *Every moment was laid out*
> *before a single day had passed.*

This confession back to our heavenly Father is submitting to the fact that He created us. My favorite part is the last two sentences of that verse because it reminds me that every moment was laid out/recorded/written in His book—before *one* of them had ever taken place. Nothing is a surprise to God. He knew you would be pregnant. He knew you when you were in your mother's belly. He is with your baby inside yours.

Inside the Womb

In your time of prayer, you'll notice that you will be praying over each organ as they are being developed. It was very interesting to read Dr. Henry Wright's book, *A More Excellent Way: Be in Health*, and discover that the connection of our physical health usually stems from a spiritual root. "Diseases in our lives can be the result of a separation from God and His Word in specific areas of our lives." If you would like to learn more on the subject of healing in spiritual areas to cure physical diseases, I would also encourage you to read Dr. M. K. Strydom's online publication, "Healing Begins with Sanctification of the Heart, No Disease Is Incurable." These two publications were two of the foundation blocks that helped me better understand why I should pray as each organ was being developed inside the womb.

Learning how sin, sickness, and disease can affect one generation after another through a spiritual disconnect (or wound) was only the beginning of my intrigue about prayer during pregnancy. What I didn't realize prior to this was how stress and trauma in the mother's life during pregnancy can also affect the baby within the womb. As the adrenal glands respond to the stress of the mother, the influx of hormonal changes enter the amniotic fluid through the umbilical cord and affects the child, who then begins to share in the stress of the mother. Any severe, long-lasting stress not tended to and dealt with by the mother during her pregnancy can imprint itself into the development of the growing fetus causing negative effects such as insecurity, lack of natural bonding with parents, or many other avoidable and destructive things throughout a child's life.

Another resource I received while preparing this prayer journal was from a colleague, "Praying for Your Unborn Child" by Francis and Judith MacNutt, only validated why I felt praying during pregnancy was so vital to the physical and spiritual health of the child, mother and entire family unit. Thus, began my own personal journey of uncovering trauma during pregnancy as far as three generations back.

The more I researched, the more I discovered that praying through the pregnancy each step of the way was confirmed by ministries tending to our spiritual health and scientific studies conducted by medical doctors tying this to our physical healing. (Please refer to the back of the book for additional healing resources.) I encourage everyone reading this book to take seriously the responsibility of pregnancy beyond exercise, regular checkups, and eating healthy. This is your moment to discover and uncover your family history, both spiritually and physically. Celebrate the godly spiritual heritage that's gone before you but also pray for healing in those areas that sin patterns or sicknesses seem to pass down generationally within your family tree. Let *your* generation be *the* generation that stands on the front lines of this spiritual battle and say, "No more. From this point forward, we will be healthy!"

Watchman on the Wall

I want to explain your position as a parent in a way that you may not have realized it before. Exodus chapter 20 tells us that the sins of the fathers are passed down to the third and fourth generation (Jeremiah 2:9), so it explains why a common disease, addiction, or tendency to bend toward particular sin patterns continues to pass throughout a family, like a contaminated baton being handed from one generation to the next. The good news is those sicknesses, diseases, and sins can be repented of and reversed, leaving behind only a legacy of health both physically and spiritually for ourselves and generations to come. However, it starts with us being accountable for our own sins and then being a "watchman on the wall" for our children and even our grandchildren, though they may not have been born yet.

I began to think about all the prayer requests we as believers, receive for people who need physical healings in their body. Sometimes this happens due to poor health choices, but other times there is a genetic predisposition that we are unaware of until it's too late. My question became, why wait until the sickness or disease shows up? Why not stop it at its onset? Why not pray very pointedly over each organ as it gets developed each week? Why not be a Watchman on the Wall for the next generation of children coming into our family and stop the enemy at his onset? It all began to make sense, read these scriptures below.

> "I have posted *watchmen on your walls,* Jerusalem; they will *never be silent* day or night. You who call on the LORD, give yourselves no rest,"
>
> —Isaiah 62:6

> "Son of man, I have made you a watchman for the people of Israel; so *hear* the word I speak and *give* them warning from me."
>
> —Ezekiel 3:17

Let's look at only what's italicized:

- Watchmen on your walls
- Never be silent
- Hear
- Give

Being *a watchman on the wall* gives someone a better vantage point to where they are looking. A watchman would often "lean in" and study the horizon to warn as early as possible at the sign of an enemy approaching camp. So as you begin to pray each week, ask the Lord to position your heart to a higher place and to open your eyes both physically and spiritually. Sometimes you may not know about a physical illness in your family but if you will be still and listen, Holy Spirit will prompt you, giving you knowledge of trauma, sicknesses or sin patterns to address that otherwise would go overlooked. When I was going through inner healing ministry back in 2010, each time we prayed over my brain I began to cry. What I later found out was that my maternal grandfather and great-grandfather both had strokes and suffered as a result of it in the latter part of their lives. So be sensitive to what God is speaking, trust what you hear and just go with it, you'll surprise yourself on how well you can hear Him speak.

Never be silent. When David ran after Goliath, he didn't do it with his mouth shut, he yelled every step of the way! Each week you are tearing down strongholds from generations past so when you pray – do it out loud. Romans 10:17 says "Faith comes by hearing, and hearing by the word of God." You'll notice a change in your own spirit as you begin speaking scripture over your baby's life! Studies show that babies in the womb can hear their parents speak to them and even recognize their voice after birth, so speak out loud as you pray each week for your baby. Sometimes it helps to place your hands on where you know your baby is positioned within your belly and imagine you were physically holding them in your arms. I wonder if you practiced this at the same time every day would your baby begin to expect this one on one time and start responding with playful kicks?

Hear. Set aside time each day to spend in prayer and ask Holy Spirit to open your ears and speak to you. I can tell you how amazing God is and how He can change your life, but when He speaks to you directly, no one can steal that from you. You will surprise yourself as He begins to lead you through prayer that you didn't know were areas of sickness. Trust that when Holy Spirit brings to memory current or past trauma, sicknesses, disease, areas of shame etc that He has done so not to bring condemnation to you but to bring healing in both your life and your baby. This will become a time of inner healing to the both of you, so be sure to journal these moments during your pregnancy.

Give. That leads to the last "charge" as a watchman on the wall and that is to give. The greatest gift you could ever give your children, even in the womb is the Word of God. Teach them that their heavenly Father is not a taskmaster waiting to strike them if they are not perfect, but a loving father who wants a relationship with them. You may have grown up in a home where you knew you were loved, but you may not have been encouraged or celebrated much less prayed over. Use these next nine months as training grounds for the next eighteen years of your child's life to give them truth from the word of God through prayer. Studies show that babies who were prayed over, celebrated and wanted in the womb grew into secure confident children. Hopefully this will become a habit that will continue every day even after they're born and for many years to come!

Your strategy is to use scriptures in practical prayers as a weapon forged to destroy any lie that would create sickness and affect your unborn child—thus breaking the hand (curse) that passes the baton to the next generation. Just remember:

"All Scripture is God-breathed and is useful for teaching, rebuking, correcting and training in righteousness,"
—1 Timothy 3:16

"No weapon forged against you will prevail, and you will refute every tongue that accuses you. This is the heritage of the servants of the LORD, and this is their vindication from me," declares the LORD."
—Isaiah 54:17

The LORD said to me, "You have seen correctly, for I am watching to see that my word is fulfilled."
—Jeremiah 1:12

Though God uses everything ultimately for His glory, it is not in His design for us to live in sickness or with the effects of trauma that may have resulted in your pregnancy, happened during your pregnancy or have been carried into your pregnancy. By praying each week of your pregnancy, you will have the opportunity to speak health over you, your unborn child, and even generations to come.

"Beloved, I wish above all things that thou mayest prosper and *be in health*, even as thy soul prospereth."
—3 John 2

LET'S GET STARTED!

The one thing you'll notice with your prayer journal is that it is simple and to the point. You'll have five questions each week that will range from a short Bible study to random questions of how your pregnancy is going thus far. Find a place each day where you can still your spirit and mind, being intentional to not only pray and journal but to train your ears to hear your heavenly Father speak to you (Isaiah 50:4). As you progress to the third trimester, you will begin decreeing and declaring God's promises to your baby. Remember that your baby's ears are fully developed and are honing in on your voice. Speak these promises out loud each day and watch how your baby will begin to respond. My prayer is that you would use this as a tool and a weapon in your hand to pray over the next generation of your family.

The prayers have been crafted to read for those of you who will wait to find out on the day of delivery if you are having a boy or girl. How exciting that you have the patience to wait for that moment, because I did not! For those of you who already know what you're going to have and have even chosen a name, I would encourage you to personalize your prayers even more by adding your baby's name where appropriate.

I would like to encourage you to visit my website www.iamlelis.com. There you will find handpicked worship songs, uplifting messages and teachings as another way for you to intentionally connect daily with your heavenly Father during this season of your life.

I am honored to have been given this assignment, and I pray that your life will not only be changed but that your sons and daughters in generations to come will emerge into their destiny and have a relationship with Christ because of the prayers you are praying today.

Be blessed!
—*Lisa Z. Blady*

Boys,

There isn't a day that goes by I don't look at the two stripes tattooed on my arm and wonder what it would be like having you with us. At the time this book releases you both would be six years old, which seems strange to think because it feels like just yesterday, we received the news that your hearts had stopped beating while you lay in your mom's belly.

Mom and I both know God's plan for you was greater than anything that we had in store, and while we wish you were here to be big brothers for your sisters, we know that you're in paradise. Lennon, Remi, and Hayes will learn all about you when they're old enough to comprehend. We can't wait to see you one day and give hugs and kisses!

Love,
Mom & Dad

ACKNOWLEDGEMENTS

Thank you, Mom and Dad, who are now both in heaven. Mom, I still remember telling the family at Easter dinner that I felt God was leading me to write a book. Your mouth dropped open, and you stared at me across the table, waiting to see if I was serious. My memories of you both are of laughter, hugs, kisses, barbeque, camping, and you yelling out the front door for us to "run home and make your beds and you better not miss the bus!" To this day I can't crawl out of my bed without making it! I can honestly say that I never saw the two of you fight or argue—I love and miss you both!

To my best friends—Lauren Trahan and Dreama Smith: Thank you for believing in me during the process of fleshing this thing out! We're still going to do the traveling prayer bus idea, I promise!

To my illustrator, Miriam Douglas, whom I practically begged to help me out: From the moment I started the book I had your artwork envisioned throughout the pages. It would not have been complete without your water color originals!

To Amanda Suanne Photography for capturing our family so beautifully: We love the front cover, and I am honored that you shared your talents on this project!

To my faithful and grounded sister in the faith, Tiffany Gautreaux: You have always amazed me with your hunger and thirst for the Word of God. God can trust you with knowledge because you never squander it or hide it for yourself. I pray that as you continue to search for it as gold that He blesses you in all areas of your life. Thank you for all that you share and for your encouraging text messages (Sozo Wholistic Wellness).

To The Kitchen Table Counseling, Marc and Melissa D'Aurnoy: Thank you for teaching me about Inner Healing and Recall Healing, pouring into me during my pain and being strong enough not to take my outbursts personally! I learned more about healing and getting to root of my trauma from "that stupid stick!" Thank you for always being willing to answer my call—I'm honored to call you my friend.

To Lennon Harper, Remi Everly, and Hayes Anna-Lynn: All I want is the best for you and for you to live out the purpose God's planted within you. I believe that you girls have been spared trauma both physically and spiritually because of the prayers we have laid up for you in heaven. You will all walk in the fullness of what God has called you to—surely goodness and mercy will go before you!

To my heavenly Father: You're right—you did make my crooked places straight! I trusted in you and was not disappointed.

"Let this be written for a future generation, that a people
not yet created may praise the Lord."

—Psalm 102:18

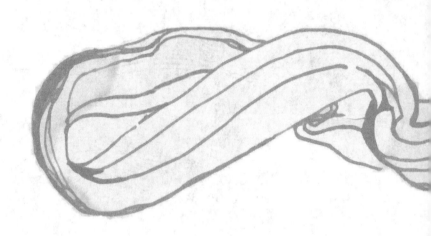

FIRST TRIMESTER
WEEKS 1–13

"In the beginning God created the heavens and the earth."
—Genesis 1:1

WEEK 1

"Lord, in view of your mercy, I lift up my body to you as a living sacrifice, holy and pleasing to you, devoted solely unto you and your service for I know this is your true and proper worship."

—*Romans 12:1–2*

DID YOU KNOW?

✓ It was once believed that women shouldn't breastfeed because the milk was too thin, but today, women are encouraged to breastfeed because of the nutrients necessary for a growing baby not found in regular milk.

✓ It was also once proper to use the phrase "expecting" rather than "pregnant."

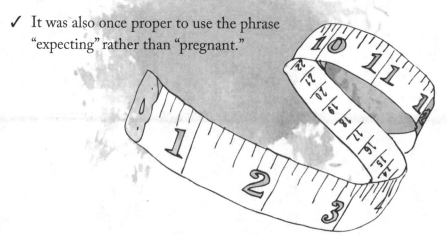

I feel the Word for this week is *prepare*. Father, as my womb is preparing to conceive, I ask that you also prepare my heart that I can be emotionally ready when the time comes for my body to carry my child for nine months. Cover and protect me and my baby during this time that this baby may grow to the fullness of all that you've created him or her to be (Ephesians 4:13).

I know there will be days when I'm overwhelmed with everything that needs to be done, so Holy Spirit, I ask that you remind me to devote myself daily to prayer and help me to remain both watchful and thankful (Colossians 4:2) that you've shared with me the privilege and honor of creating life. I surrender my life to you, Jesus, and ask that you come and live inside my heart (Romans 10:9). Forgive me for the life that I've led up until this day, and help me to be a godly woman, a loving mother, and an example of Christ to my children.

(Pause and reflect on your past relationship with God, and ask Him to put His finger on areas where you should ask for forgiveness. Then confess your sin, ask for forgiveness and repent. Please refer to the back of the book for a prayer that will help lead you through repentence.)

Lord, just as you prepare the soil of the ground for the seed to be received and grow into its purpose, you are preparing my womb to receive the seed of *life*. Father, everything you prepare is a good thing and has a purpose, so I am putting my trust in you, and when the season of my life is right, you will bless me with a child—and my baby will be dedicated to you and serve you all the days of his or her life (1 Samuel 1:9–28).

Being Still

Day 1
What are your thoughts on being pregnant at this point of your life?

Day 2
When your mother was your age did she have children? How many?

Day 3
How big do you think your family will be?

Day 4

When do you think life begins in the womb? At conception? At the first heartbeat? Have you ever given it much thought?

Day 5

How could you prepare your body, your spirit, your emotions, and your mental state for potential pregnancy and family?

Your word is strong and powerful and able to tear down strongholds. Father, let none of Your words I speak over myself and my child fall to the ground and die but that they would fall on a fertile heart that is rich with confidence, trusting that you will do what you say. Amen.

WEEK 2

"Listen to me, all you in distant lands! Pay attention, you who are far away! The LORD called me before my birth; from within the womb He called me by name. He made my words of judgment as sharp as a sword. He has hidden me in the shadow of his hand. I am like a sharp arrow in his quiver."

—*Isaiah 49:1–2*

DID YOU KNOW?

✓ During the first two weeks of your pregnancy your body is preparing for fertilization.

✓ It is recommended that you take folic acid daily; it'll protect the development of your child's brain.

Lord, continue tilling up the soil of my heart as you prepare its ground to receive truth. Remove any stones (which are lies embedded in my thinking) that may make its way into another generation of my family. Let it start with me, Father; open my eyes to see you in a new way and hear you in a new way that I might respond with a grateful heart, knowing that you never expose anything in my life out of condemnation but out of compassion to be drawn closer to you and to be set free from chains of bondage.

Father, I am amazed that before I even conceive my child, you already know his or her name and have created this baby for victory—not defeat. Your greatness amazes me, and even though I cannot fully understand how you will form this tiny baby in my womb (Ecclesiastes 11:5), I am humbled that you would bless me with the honor of carrying a child. Whether this pregnancy was planned or unexpected, I believe that life begins at conception, and it is never our right to take a life, even an unborn baby—at any time during a pregnancy. You love me, and you love this child. In this you will have a purpose for us both, so I trust you in all things: your timing, my family, and my future. Father, prepare both my heart and my womb to receive the seed of life and this journey.

Search me out, Lord, and know my heart, see if there is any vile thing about me (Psalm 139:23). I am a person with unclean hands and unclean lips (Isaiah 6:1), so wash me with your forgiveness (John 15:3) as I repent from living apart from you (Psalm 51), and lift up holy hands for you to anoint them (1 Timothy 2:8). I commit to teaching my children that they were created in your image and their identity comes from you and not what the world, television, social media, or their own failures say about them (1 John 3:1).

Being Still

Day 1
Read Luke 1:26–45. What about this passage of scripture stands out that you've never noticed before?

Day 2
Imagine today if you were visited by an angel, telling you that you would become pregnant. What reasons might you come up with about why you wouldn't be equipped to be a mother or why being pregnant right now is bad timing?

Day 3
In verses 39–45, the scriptures say that Mary went very quickly to see Elizabeth. This friendship was appointed, in advance by God. What godly friendship do you have in your life that you can run to during these next nine months?

Day 4

Verse 37 says, "For with God nothing will be impossible." Scripture was referring to Elizabeth being barren in her old age, yet she was still pregnant. What are you carrying right now that seems impossible for anyone, even God?

Day 5

Read Luke 1:26–45 again. This time ask the Holy Spirit to reveal something new to you, and see what stands out. Journal that, even if it seems small and insignificant.

"For his invisible attributes, namely, his eternal power and divine nature, have been clearly perceived, ever since the creation of the world, in the things that have been made. So they are without excuse."

—Romans 1:20

WEEK 3

"Then God said, "Let us make mankind
in our image, in our likeness."

—*Genesis 1:26*

DID YOU KNOW?

✓ God has already determined the sex of
your child at conception.

✓ Cells developing this week are the size
of a pinhead.

✓ For the next six days, the blastocyst will
travel down the fallopian tube to settle
into your uterine wall.

Okay, I'm pregnant! Breathe. Breathe. Help me, Father, to take a deep breath and process what just happened. How can this be? Regardless of whether this is planned or not, I've partnered with heaven and created—a miracle.

Father, you are so intimately acquainted with us even at the very DNA structure of our bodies. It is a miracle that one cell will multiply exponentially in the days, weeks, and months to come and form a living and breathing human being!

I've only been pregnant a few days, and the genetic makeup is already forming, from the personality, hair color, and physical appearance to, most importantly, the sex of the baby. God, you did not make a mistake! I'm crying out to you right now, Father! Help me to slow down and see this baby as a child, as a human, as a world changer—as a miracle! Rescue my heart from chains and lies, from darkness and fear—I lift up my hands—help me!

My child, from the first day I knew I was pregnant; I haven't stopped thanking God and will not stop praying for you. I am asking God to give you a wise mind and spirit attuned to His will, to acquire a thorough understanding of the ways in which He works. I will pray that you'll live well for the Master, making Him proud of you as you work hard in all things. As you learn more and more how God works, you will learn how to walk in your calling. I pray that you'll have the strength to stick it out over the long haul—not the grim strength of gritting your teeth but the glory-strength God gives. It is strength that endures the unendurable and spills over into joy, thanking our Father who makes us strong enough to take part in everything bright and beautiful that He has for us. (Colossians 1:9–14)

Being Still

Day 1

Go to my website www.iamlelis.com and watch this week's video. At the twenty-seven second mark, did you notice the explosion of light erupt when the sperm enters the egg? Spend some quiet time reflecting on that. Does that cause you to look at conception differently?

Day 2

Now read Ephesians 5:8 in the margin. Do you see God at the core of your child's creation differently? This is a milestone in your life, whether you realize it or not. Journal your thoughts that you can later share with your child at a milestone in their life.

Day 3

God created all things and yet chose you to co-labor with Him in the creation of your child. Write a prayer, thanking God for allowing Him to share with you in the creation of life.

Day 4
Read 2 Corinthians 4:6 and watch the video again. How does the sperm creating a spark of light on entering the egg relate to this verse where God is saying, "Light shall shine out of darkness"? Meditate on this, and journal what God is speaking to you.

Day 5
If your pregnancy wasn't planned but was the result of an unfortunate instance, how does seeing this week's video and relating it to 1 John 1:5 bring comfort to your situation?

"For you were once darkness, but now you are light in the Lord. Live as children of light."

—*Ephesians 5:8*

WEEK 4

*"You made all the delicate, inner parts of my body and knit
them together in my mother's womb. Thank you for making
me so wonderfully complex! It is amazing to think about. Your
workmanship is marvelous—and how well I know it. You
were there while I was being formed in utter seclusion! You saw
me before I was born and scheduled each day of my life before
I began to breathe. Every day was recorded in your book!"*
—*Psalm 139:13–16 MSG*

DID YOU KNOW?

✓ Your baby is smaller than a poppy seed.

✓ Three layers of cells are now developing. The inner layer will
be the digestive system, liver, and lungs.

✓ The middle layer will be the heart, sex organs, bones, kidneys,
and muscles.

✓ The outer layer will be the nervous system,
hair, skin, and eyes.

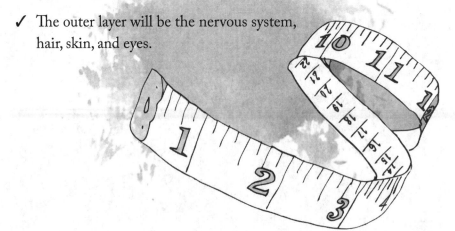

I'm speechless, Father; I'm truly speechless. I've never thought about how complex our human bodies are and how much detail went into how you created us. I've taken for granted life itself, and ask that you forgive me for never submitting to your love and in return receiving your unselfish love toward me. I myself am fearfully and wonderfully made, and I celebrate myself today (Psalm 139:14)! Open up my heart these next nine months, so I understand the depths of my own creation and fall in love with the intricacies of how you create life! You are like no other!

This week, the cells are dividing into three layers to create the digestive system, liver, lungs, heart, reproductive organs, bones, kidneys, muscles, nervous system, hair, skin, and eyes. They are all operating and working together in a space as small as a poppy seed! How can it be?

I am a masterpiece! I commit to you right now that I will take care of my body so that my baby has a healthy home in which to grow these next nine months. I put aside all selfish ambition and commit to eat healthy food, exercise daily, and pray over the continued growth of my child. I pray that this little one will also have a desire to eat well and will see his or her body as a temple of the Holy Spirit, useful for His good works (1 Corinthians 6:19–20; Ephesians 4:12). Father, I put away all selfishness within me and like my baby will crave milk—I crave spiritual food (1 Peter 2:1–2). Just as Jewish tradition led Mary to seek out Elizabeth (Luke 1:56-67), I ask that you bring godly women into my life that can speak truth and love (Hebrews 4:15) over me so that I learn to hear your voice (John 10:27) more clearly and lay the foundation (Hebrews 6:1) for a healthy and safe life for my child.

Being Still

Day 1

Have you ever seen the size of a poppy seed? Your baby is smaller than that seed. Journal what thoughts go through your mind as you meditate on everything that God is creating in such a microscopic space.

Day 2

What steps might you begin taking to find godly women to lean on during these next nine months? Write your own personal prayer to God, asking Him to meet this need.

Day 3

Develop a practical exercise program that is simple yet challenging enough that you can be dedicated to it each week. Start today!

Day 4

Why do you think God is so concerned about our physical health as much as he's concerned about our spiritual health?

Day 5

Have you shared your pregnancy with anyone? Why or why not?

"Don't you realize that your body is the temple of the Holy Spirit, who lives in you and was given to you by God? You do not belong to yourself, for God bought you with a high price. So you must honor God with your body."

—1 Corinthians 6:19

WEEK 5

"Before I formed you in the womb I knew you, before you were born I set you apart; I appointed you as a prophet to the nations."

—Jeremiah 1:5

DID YOU KNOW?

✓ Your baby is the size of an apple seed or peppercorn.

✓ The heart and circulatory are developing.

✓ Your baby's heart has two tiny channels.

✓ The brain, spinal cord, heart, and blood vessels are starting to form.

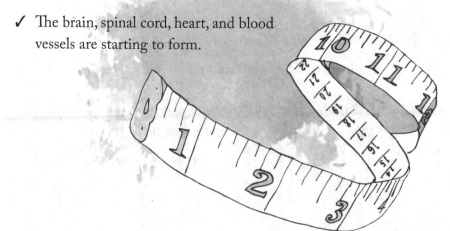

This week, twenty-two days after conception, the cells have formed from a tube to a loop, and my child's heart has already started beating! As the neural tubes start to close and the brain begins to develop into three areas, I know you are watching as this unformed substance begins to take shape (Psalm 139:16). It's amazing how each cell follows the instructions you've assigned it. As my child's spinal cord begins to close and form, I speak over my baby's body that the spine will grow straight, its brain will divide properly into the forebrain, midbrain and hindbrain, and that nothing would be lacking during this time of development.

I'm believing you, Father, for a strong heart and healthy brain and cancel any previous dysfunction that may have been in my bloodline up until this point. Lord, I seek you every day and trust that my child's health is in your hands. If my baby is lacking anything during this time of development that would cause him or her to suffer or not form the way you have created each organ to form, I ask that you would do a creative miracle in my womb today. Lead me each week, Father, to hear your voice, so I would know if there is any area during my pregnancy that you would ask me to pray over.

Mold my heart to see this child as a living, breathing human being and not just a "mass of cells" inside my body that can be easily discarded. Break my heart for what breaks yours, and teach me to trust you that I am going to be better because I trust you for my future (Psalm 22:5).

Being Still

Day 1

Go to my website www.iamlelis.com and watch this week's video. How did your view of God change when you learned about the structure of our DNA and Laminin?

Day 2

Louie Giglio explains how God wrote who you were ordained to be with the three billion characters within your DNA, creating you to be someone that no one has ever been created to be in the history of humankind. Write a prayer back to God, thanking Him for loving you and asking Him to reveal to you the gifts and purposes He created within you.

Day 3

Regardless of whether your pregnancy was planned or a mistake, what joy can you find in the honor God has given you with sharing in the creation of life?

Day 4

Just a few short days ago, your body started the creation process with one small cell and now is exponentially multiplying each day. Have you ever considered yourself a miracle? What unique qualities of yourself would you like to see passed down to your child?

Day 5

How are you going to see yourself and your child differently now that you've learned that God is in the core of your DNA structure?

"Through him God created everything in the heavenly realms and on earth. He made the things we can see and the things we can't see—such as thrones, kingdoms, rulers, and authorities in the unseen world. Everything was created through him and for him. He existed before anything else, and he holds all creation together.

—Colossians 1:16-17 NLT

WEEK 6

"He makes the whole body fit together perfectly. As each part does its own special work, it helps the other parts grow, so that the whole body is healthy and growing and full of love."

—*Ephesians 4:16*

DID YOU KNOW?

✓ Your baby is the size of a sweet pea.

✓ Your baby's face is beginning to take shape.

✓ Your baby's heart is starting to beat regularly at 110 beats/minutes.

✓ Dimples are starting to form on the side of the head to prepare for ears, eyes, and nose.

Father, in such a short amount of time, my baby has already tripled in size, and the heart is beating at a steady rhythm to move the blood through all the organs. You've placed dimples for the ear canals on the sides of the head and a place marker where the eyes and nose will appear on the face. As the kidneys, liver, and lungs begin to form under my baby's transparent skin only one cell thick, I pray health and strength over each organ. You created our organs to function in a special role so that our bodies would fit together, work, and grow strong.

As my body begins to adapt to the changes going on internally, I ask that you would make me strong and fit to carry this baby full term. I will not focus my eyes on the things that could go wrong or have gone wrong in the past, but I keep my eyes on the cross and renew my mind and heart daily to trust you (Romans 12:2). I will not take the easy way out and abort this pregnancy; I will shut my ears to the lion that roars inside my head, making me feel pressured to follow my own prescribed, short-sided plan for my life. I will lift up my hands again and again this week, as often as I have to as an act of surrender of trusting you, so I don't create plans of destruction (Proverbs 14:1).

Father, you have given me this child to carry, and I will continue to hold on to the hope that my baby is growing healthy and being covered and protected in my womb. I will not fear a miscarriage because you have not placed fear inside my heart—but a confident heart that will not faint (2 Timothy 1:7).

Everything you do has a purpose. Emotions don't determine whether we are a boy or a girl, the God of creation does. Even though it will not be revealed to us for another sixteen weeks, the gender of my baby is no surprise to you, and I pray my child would not be deceived into thinking that you made a mistake. I break that lie now from ever forming in the name of Jesus.

Being Still

Day 1

You may have just found out that you are pregnant. Where were you when you found out, who were you with, and what was your initial reaction? Be honest.

Day 2

How long did it take the news to settle? Journal all the thoughts that were going through your mind? Were you scared? Were you elated?

Day 3

Spend some time today and write your new little one a letter. Then seal it and put it away until an age-appropriate time. Also make a habit of creating a weekly note for your child in an entirely new journal.

Day 4

If God could write a letter to you about your being pregnant, what would He say? Be honest with yourself.

Day 5

As you and God co-labor to create your child, what character traits would you like them to have? What do you see as your part in the process, and what do you see as God's?

"Thus says the Lord, who made you and formed you from the womb, who will help you."

—Isaiah 44:2

WEEK 7

"For he has strengthened the bars of your gates;
he has blessed your children within you."

—*Psalm 147:13*

DID YOU KNOW?

✓ Your baby is the size of a blueberry or coffee bean.

✓ The kidneys are now in place and will begin to produce urine.

✓ Your baby's hands are like a paddle and will begin to develop more as weeks progress.

Father, I find peace and comfort in knowing that my child is blessed even within my womb and that receiving blessings from you require first my heart and my trust in you. Your word is scattered with promises where you say that you show your love and covenant to a thousand generations to those who keep your commandments (Exodus 20:6). Father, I want to be a woman after your heart! I may not do everything right, but I want to always please you so that my children will sit under the blessings of your hand and the shadow of your wing (Psalm 91:1). How could I have ever doubted that you were incapable to handle my real-life problems when you are the author and creator of life itself (Hebrews 12:2)?

Some inherited diseases are stemmed from a spiritually rooted sin in our own life or from generations before us (Exodus 20:5–6). Fear of any kind has been found to cause sickness in the kidneys, so as you are creating and developing my child's kidneys this week, I repent for any fear that has been tolerated in my family line—terror, fright, paranoia, horror, or exposure to violence. I cast them down and cover myself and generations to come with the blood of Christ, leaving only a legacy of peace and hope.

I pray that my child's kidneys will properly process the food that my body will transfer through my umbilical cord—only eighteen inches away. As the brain cells are forming one hundred per minute within my child who is the size of a blueberry, I pray order and precision to each one! You are a God of detail and are concerned with every intricate part of our lives (Psalm 37:23). Will I ever stop being amazed at how great you are? You say we are worth more than the sparrow, yet you feed them and provide shelter to rest their head, so I trust that my baby will grow healthy, and you will continue to provide for our needs (Matthew 6:26).

Being Still

Day 1

Just as the kidney's filter impurities from harming the body, what things would you ask God to filter from your life to prevent harmful consequences affecting your child (i.e., past emotional, physical, or spiritual)?

Day 2

Ask God to show you what being a mother after His heart would look like and to bring godly influential people into your life to mentor you through this season of your life.

Day 3

Go to my website www.iamlelis.com and watch this week's video. Spend this time sitting with your eyes closed and just relax, listening to the music. Then watch the video again and journal anything that stands out more than the other.

Day 4

Watch the video for this week again. Read Jeremiah 1:5 and meditate on that verse. What does *sanctify* mean? How do you see that God has sanctified your life?

Day 5

All of creation began when a sperm fertilized an oocyte cell, becoming a zygote cell. Creation began at conception. Does that change how you view life? Journal your thoughts.

It was common Jewish custom for a pregnant woman to seek out other women to assist with the burdens of pregnancy and prepare themselves for the coming baby. Even in today's society Jewish customs encourage the woman to create a healthy emotional and physical surrounding for the fetus to develop. Read how Mary sought after Elizabeth during this time in her life.

—Luke 1:56-67

WEEK 8

"But the angel said to him: "Do not be afraid, Zechariah; your prayer has been heard. Your wife Elizabeth will bear you a son, and you are to call him John."

—Luke 1:13

DID YOU KNOW?

✓ Your baby is the size of a large raspberry.

✓ The intestines will move to the umbilical cord and begin to develop.

✓ Your baby's genitals are developed.

✓ The heart is now divided into the right and left chambers.

Father, I have to admit that when I first heard those words confirming that I was indeed pregnant, every thought from joy to fear came through my mind (John 14:27). I don't know the path of the wind, or how a body is formed in my womb, so I cannot understand the work of God, the Maker of all things (Ecclesiastes 11:5). All I can do is smile when I visualize that my tiny baby is the size of a large raspberry this week, and the intestines are moving from the body into the umbilical cord to develop out of the cramped quarters of my womb. Father, watch over that short journey and allow my body to accept this process and aid my child's organs in developing to their fullness.

Holy Spirit, begin to overflow and pour into the chambers of my child's heart as it begins to divide from the left to the right. While you begin separating each chamber of my baby's heart, search my own heart and divide those things that would separate me from you (Psalm139:23–24). Your word says that a merry heart does good like a medicine but a broken spirit dries up the bones (Proverbs 17:22). Help me to be still. Be still. Breathe in. Breathe out. Holy Spirit, show me brokenness in my own heart so that I can deal with any sadness, anger, bitterness, disappointment, or abandonment I feel, so it is not transferred to my child as the bones begin to develop this week. As those bones and muscles grow stronger, so let my child's spirit grow stronger and never be intimidated by tactics of the enemy.

I am only eight weeks pregnant and already my baby's webbed hands, though small like tiny paddles, are being trained for battle even in the womb (Psalm 18:34). Father, let the battle never be against you or other godly influences in their life. Give my child discernment to know when to use their hands for healing and when to use them to bring down unrighteous structures.

Being Still

Day 1
This week, your embryo has grown into a fetus. The meaning of the Latin word fetus is "offspring." What is the definition of offspring?

Day 2
Even though you are very early in your pregnancy, do you feel comfortable saying that you are "pregnant with a child"?

Day 3
Do you see yourself changing any eating habits, social habits, or even physical exercise now that you are pregnant?

Day 4
Early in the pregnancy, it's common to need power naps in the middle of the afternoon. How have your sleeping patterns been this week?

Day 5
What changes in your body have you started noticing this week?

"For behold, from now on all generations will call me blessed. For He who is mighty has done great things for me and holy is his name.."
(Mary, singing a song to God for blessing her with a child)
—*Luke 1:48–49 ESV*

WEEK 9

"I trust in you."

—Psalm 25:2

DID YOU KNOW?

✓ Your baby is the size of a green olive.

✓ Your baby's heart now has four chambers and is audible with an ultrasound.

✓ The bladder and urethra leave the umbilical cord to go *back* into your baby's abdomen because now there's enough space.

Trust—*trust?* Even when I don't see? I guess that's what trust is, isn't it, Lord? I've been hurt before when I trusted, so how can I be vulnerable to a God I can't see when the people I do see have hurt me? I'm learning, and I'm trying. Help me to stop closing doors and show me how to tear down those walls I've put up that separate me from the people I love and who love me.

Father, we are a spirit living in a body that has a soul (mind, will, and emotions). Some diseases we carry in our body have been embedded into our DNA and act as an open door from one generation to the next. So this week, as the gallbladder, liver, and spleen begin to form inside my baby's one-inch petite frame, I pray over any physical or spiritual abnormalities that these organs may have in their DNA that would have been passed through conception.

Father, I repent from all anger, slander, bitterness, and filthy language that I have ever said or held against anyone and release them from any hurt they may have caused me, and I trust in *you* to be my rear guard and defender (Isaiah 58:8). I don't want to take any of this ungodly behavior any further in my life and through this pregnancy.

I ask that you forgive me and help me to walk in a way that would bring you glory (Colossians 3:8; James 1:20). I know that these things open the door for the enemy and also sickness that can dwell in our bodies, so I rebuke and cancel anything that may have been transferred onto my baby from generations past. I declare love, joy, peace, patience, kindness, goodness, faithfulness, gentleness, and self-control over my baby and the righteous fruit that would stem from this during development (Galatians 5:22).

Being Still

Day 1

I trust you. Do you remember a time when you trusted everyone? When you trusted no one? Journal events that happened in the gap that brought the mistrust.

Day 2

What could you do to create an environment of trust for your child? As we think about the new life inside, it's not uncommon to feel anxious or fearful. Yet, you can trust that God will lead you as you seek him as this new life grows.

Day 3

In what ways could you honor your baby as you carry them during these nine months of pregnancy?

Day 4
You may be able to hear your baby's heartbeat this week. Have you scheduled your next appointment? Have you already heard the heart beat? How were you feeling when you first heard another life coming from your belly?

Day 5
Have you started showing this week? How do you feel about your body?

"Abraham believed God, and it was accounted to him for righteousness."

—*Romans 4:3*

WEEK 10

"And I heard a loud voice from the throne saying,
"Look! God's dwelling place is now among the
people, and he will dwell with them.:

—*Revelation 21:3*

DID YOU KNOW?

✓ Your baby is the size of a prune.

✓ Your baby's fingers and toes begin to form.

✓ The testes are producing testosterone.

✓ The stomach is producing digestive juice.

✓ Arms are beginning to flex.

Dwelling place. Oh how I love those two words together. A dwelling is a place of residency. Place is a particular position. You are taking up residence in a very specific position of my body—my womb. It sounds like such a safe and comfortable place to be that I wish at times I could curl up with my baby and reside there. Then I could always be at peace.

Father, I place my hand on my belly and come into agreement with Your word that you would cover my child, and I say that this is a safe place inside my womb. I rest in knowing that I have the authority by your word to cancel any previous birth defects or abnormalities that may have risen (remained/carried) in my blood line that would try to move to the next generation. I renew my mind daily so that I can live in peace and know your perfect will for my life (Romans 12:2), and I release forgiveness and wholesome speech to everyone who would hear me speak—especially my child (Ephesians 4:29) so that no toxic word would take root into another generation.

This is the day that the Lord has made (Psalm 118:24); this week as the stomach begins producing digestive juices, I speak health and order over it, declaring that no root of dread or fear of the future will attach itself to my baby! As the kidneys begin to produce urine and become a filter from impurities for the body so toxins will not be allowed to stay in the blood stream, I pray that the Word of God would also be a filter of truth for my child. As your word gets stronger, I pray it would prevent and sift out any lie before it enters the ear gates and has the opportunity to cause long-term disease and develop a pattern of destruction. I pray complete wholeness in all areas.

Being Still

Day 1
Too many expectant moms focus on the sickness or discomfort. What joy can you discover in the discomfort of this season?

Day 2
Read the scripture below. What kind of dwelling place do you think God would want to live in?

Day 3
Read the scripture below. If God is in heaven, why does He want to make a dwelling place in you?

Day 4

Your baby's kidneys are developing this week. Their purpose is to remove toxins and protect the body. Spend some quiet time with God and ask the Holy Spirit to put His finger on what toxic people, activities, behaviors, or thoughts need to be removed from your life.

Day 5

Have you had to start adjusting your clothes to fit better or begin to wear loose-fitting jeans?

"You also are being built together for a dwelling place of God in the Spirit."

—Ephesians 2:22

WEEK 11

"But the LORD said to Samuel, "Do not consider his appearance or his height, for I have rejected him. The LORD does not look at the things people look at. People look at the outward appearance, but the LORD looks at the heart."

—*1 Samuel 16:7*

DID YOU KNOW?

✓ Your baby is the size of a lime.

✓ Your baby's ovaries are developing.

✓ Ears are beginning to appear.

✓ The nasal passages are opening, the tongue and palate are forming, and hair follicles are showing up.

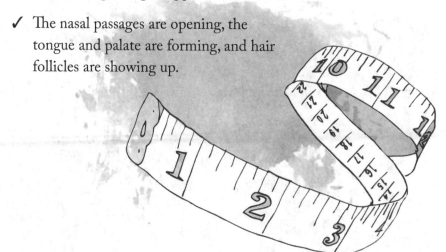

The fruit a lie can produce is a harvest that yields years of insecurity, anger, and never feeling like you're enough. The seed of the lie is rooted deep, and its tentacles demand control of everything the ear gates hear, twisting the heart to believe that everything it speaks is reality. If not dealt with, a lie can lead to a host of diseases rooting in the very things that are developing this week. Oh, but *God*!

My precious baby is two inches long this week—wow, two inches! Father, I lift up the nasal passages and developing ovaries (if I am carrying a little girl), and I believe for health and complete wholeness. I pray for strength and rebuke any rebelliousness that would try to root itself into the bones to prevent them from hardening this week or act as a destructive seed that would lay dormant and cause problems later in life. I pray that, as my baby's heart beats, it would stay in tune with yours, always remaining moldable and pliable, willing to obey when you speak. I lift up my child's ears as they begin to develop and say that they would only hear the voice of our Father, the voice of the enemy they would not follow (John 10:5). I repent over my own heart and rebellious behavior and ask that you would forgive me, change my heart, and show me how to change to become more like you daily (Ezekiel 18:31).

Father, hold my baby's hands as they are being formed this week, and put your fingerprints onto their fingerprints, inscribe their name into the palm of your hand, and write it on your heart so that you would never forget us (Isaiah 49:16). *We are children of the King*!

Being Still

Day 1

Are you holding unforgiveness against others? Yourself? Spend a few moments alone and ask your heavenly Father to show you specifically; then ask for forgiveness and healing from the pain it has left behind. Don Dickerman is a legendary pastor who writes about unforgiveness and its role in allowing generational curses to pass down. In his book, *When Pigs Move In*, Don urges Christians to forgive. Who do you need to forgive, today?

Day 2

Imagine for a moment your grandchildren—I know it's difficult because it seems almost impossible to think that far ahead—but God is already planning for it. What legacy of relationship with Christ would you like to leave for them to walk in?

Day 3

Still imagining that God is already preparing your baby's next generation even before they're born, what advice would you give your child as he or she prepares for parenthood?

Day 4

Read 2 Timothy 1:5 below. Do you recognize a sincere faith or lack of faith in your mother and/or grandmother that you may be carrying out in your life? How can you continue on or remove the unbelief from your own life to pass down to your unborn baby to walk in?

Day 5

Creating memorable moments with your children can be a great way to strengthen a family and give them a sense of belonging and security. What family tradition can you begin that would be small and simple enough to continue for years to come?

"I am reminded of your sincere faith, which first lived in your grandmother Lois and in your mother Eunice and, I am persuaded, now lives in you also."

—*2 Timothy 1:5 (NIV)*

WEEK 12

"Whoever dwells in the shelter of the Most High will rest in the shadow of the Almighty. I will say of the LORD, 'He is my refuge and my fortress, my God, in whom I trust. Surely he will save you from the fowler's snare and from the deadly pestilence. He will cover you with his feathers, and under his wings you will find refuge; his faithfulness will be your shield and rampart.'"

—Psalm 91:1–4

DID YOU KNOW?

✓ Your baby is the size of a small plum.

✓ The pituitary gland begins to develop, so your baby can make babies one day.

✓ The digestive system begins to practice moving, so food can be processed.

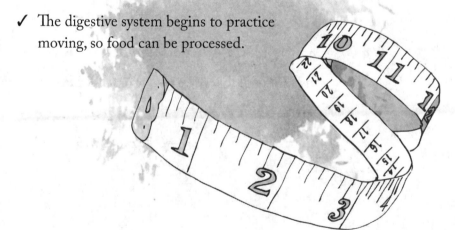

Father, I release trauma passed down our family line that has been stored within our DNA and cancel any effect that it would have on my unborn baby. Just as Ezekiel spoke and prophesied to the many dry bones to live (Ezekiel 37:2), I speak strength and order to the white blood cells that are forming this week and say that the number of cells required for my child's body to fight disease are perfect, healthy, and adequate in *quantity*—lacking in nothing.

I repent from every time I've looked to someone or something else to be accepted and validated. Your word enough brings life to my spirit and nourishes me when I am without hope and in despair; without it I would perish and live empty. Father, as your word is food to my spirit, what I eat is food to my body. Help me to be conscience of the food I eat so that it brings nourishment to my body and developing baby. I lift up the digestive tract that is also forming this week and pray that as I continue to eat healthy food, the organs would be properly trained to process and retain its nutrients.

Lord, even in this early stage in my womb, you are preparing the next generation of children in our family as the pituitary glands begin to form within my child. I speak a legacy of honor and declare that my children and their children will be established before you (Psalm 102:28), and they will praise you as long as they live (Psalm 146:2). My grandchildren will rise up and call their parents blessed and will honor you (Proverbs 31:28) all the days of their lives; they will live long in the promises you have for them (Exodus 20:12).

Being Still

Day 1

What commitment are you making to yourself and your baby with healthy eating habits during your pregnancy?

Day 2

Can you think of any trauma that you noticed keeps getting passed down to each generation—both your family's and your child's father's family? Bring it to God and ask Him to heal it.

Day 3

Write out a prayer that your child can pray over their child—your grandchild—during pregnancy that can be a legacy you would like to leave behind.

Day 4

Go to my website www.iamlelis.com and watch this week's video. As you listen to the lyrics of the song, what verse speaks the loudest to you about how you feel about God? Write a prayer to God describing how you feel about Him this week.

Day 5

What do you think God wants to tell you as He keeps you hidden either in this season of your life or at an earlier time when you know He's protected you?

Trust you completely, I'm listening intently—you'll

guide me through these many shadows.

—Lyrics from "Hidden" by Will Reagan

WEEK 13

*"And in him you too are being built together to become
a dwelling in which God lives by his Spirit."*

—*Ephesians 2:22*

DID YOU KNOW?

✓ Your baby is the size of a peach and
three inches long.

✓ The intestines are now moving from
the umbilical cord back into your baby's
abdomen.

✓ The vocal cords are now developing.

✓ Your baby can move their thumb into
the mouth.

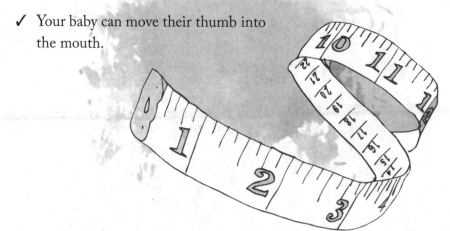

Father, in You I trust. I'm learning firsthand the magnitude of what you are creating, and I am honored to stand alongside your promises as you fashion my precious little baby in a secret place. *Your* eyes are the only ones that have protected and watched over my child during these first three months of my pregnancy—your Spirit is our Comforter.

A few weeks ago, my baby's intestines moved into my umbilical cord to begin developing, and this week, they return to my child's abdomen. I know that just as your amazing hands have set the stars in place and hung them on nothing (Psalm 8:3), you will place each organ perfectly where it's been assigned and command that they function in the way you have created them to function. As in heaven it shall be on earth, and at the name of Jesus every knee shall bow, my child's body will receive instructions from you and yield to your command (Matthew 6:9–13; Philippians 2:10).

As my baby's vocal cords are developing this week, I pray that the cartridge, lining, and ligaments would grow and form properly in the throat. Psalm 141:3 says "Set a guard over my mouth and keep watch over the door of my lips." Lord, create a sensitive heart so that before any words come forth from my child's mouth, they would first be dealt with in the heart, and your response would always be (2 Corinthians 1:20) *yes* and *amen!* Let my child be someone who always uses wisdom in life and is known for having a voice that would break silence, standing up for injustice and speaking truth and righteousness even when it's not popular.

Even though my baby's eyes are closed shut, I know they are fixed on you! I pray they would always look to you and not things in the world and will always recognize your presence in everything.

Being Still

Day 1
As you are finishing your first trimester, your sleepiness and morning sickness should soon begin to subside. Journal how you have been feeling lately and what you've been doing to get through these last few weeks.

Day 2
Have you had your first ultrasound yet? What were your thoughts when you first laid eyes on your baby?

Day 3
Your child's body is so small that the organs have had to relocate into your umbilical cord in order to continue to grow. How does that change your view of pregnancy? Are you beginning to see it more of a miracle?

Day 4
Read Isaiah 50:4. What would you have to change in your life in order to hear from God every morning?

Day 5
As you wrap up your first trimester this week, write a short note to your baby describing your feelings about his or her anticipated arrival.

"The Sovereign Lord has given me a well-instructed tongue, to know the word that sustains the weary. He wakens me morning by morning, wakens my ear to listen like one being instructed."

—Isaiah 50:4 NIV

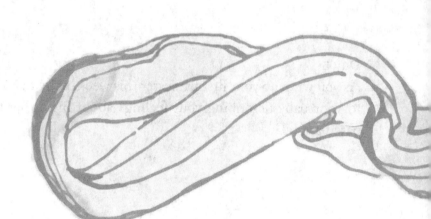

SECOND TRIMESTER
WEEKS 14–27

"Thus says the LORD, your Redeemer who formed
you from the womb: "I am the LORD, who has made
all things, who alone stretched out the heavens, who by
Myself spread out the earth,"

—Isaiah 44:24

WEEK 14

*"And in him you too are being built together to become
a dwelling in which God lives by his Spirit."*

—*Ephesians 2:22*

DID YOU KNOW?

✓ Your baby is the size of a fist and four
inches long.

✓ Your baby's genitals are *fully formed*.

✓ Your baby is developing reflexes to loud
noises and making facial muscles to
practice smiling and frowning.

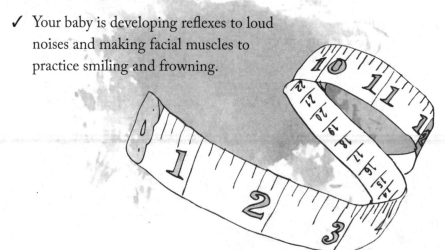

Father, as I begin my second trimester, the front portion of the brain divides into two hemispheres, each controlling the opposite side of the body. As a potter marks the clay and how lifting weights sculpt muscles—sculpt my baby's brain with a precise measure of accuracy. I speak life, strength, and health over this baby as activity begins to increase in the brain and say wake up! Increase brain health! Let no trauma from generations past attach itself to him or her. Increase and expand the brain's ability to learn and retain information! Place your hands over the neural tubes, so they form properly, and this baby will be able to think and move with coordination after he or she is born. I pray peace over my own mind throughout the day and declare that I will rest in peace during this pregnancy.

I also pray over the genitals as they begin to form this week. Father, you have made no mistake in determining the sex of this baby. I refuse to allow any lie that the enemy may use through trauma and emotional pain to confuse my child into believing he or she is the opposite gender from that which you have created. I cancel every assignment from the pit of hell that would attempt to come forth in one more generation and steal the identity of my baby, your child.

I lift up the muscles in this baby's face and body and I'm thankful that he or she is learning how to turn and twist inside my belly. Strengthen my baby in the small things he or she is doing so that in the weeks to come, their muscles will be able to stretch, pull, tug, and kick.

Being Still

Day 1

Read Jeremiah 1:5 below. What are your thoughts about God having already determined the sex of your child at conception?

Day 2

How will you handle a situation of someone who's teaching your child that they are neither a boy nor a girl?

Day 3

Meditate on 2 Corinthians 6:18. What is God trying to say to you in that scripture? Do you sense that God is delighted in you when He says He will be your father? How do you perceive this heavenly view of you?

Day 4
Your baby can start detecting loud noises from inside your belly and can even be startled if they're loud enough. Have you noticed any jumps during those loud moments lately?

Day 5
Now that most of the morning sickness has started to subside, what crazy foods have you started craving?

"Before I formed you in the womb I knew you, before you were born I set you apart; I appointed you as a prophet to the nations."

—Jeremiah 1:5 NIV

WEEK 15

But blessed are your eyes for they see, and your ears for they hear.
—*Matthew 13:16*

DID YOU KNOW?

✓ Your baby is the size of a naval orange and weighs two ounces.

✓ Your baby's skeleton is starting to ossify.

✓ Your baby's ears are moving from the side of the neck and eyes from the side of the head to the correct positions.

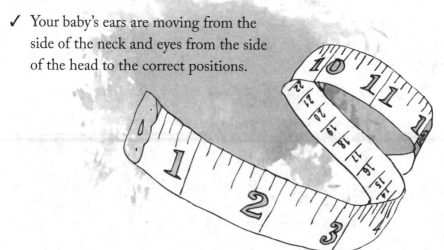

Father, bless the relationship between my baby and me as he or she grows from childhood to an adult so that when the struggles and challenges of life come, this new life will have confidence to know that I am grounded in you. There will never be a day that my baby would feel insecure and not trust that all of his or her needs are being met. I pray my baby's eyes would always be focused on you during times when feeling outnumbered and overwhelmed; remind this baby always, Father, that there are more on our side than are against us (2 King 6:16). I pray that the physical development of his or her eyes would form perfectly and cancel any previous deformities that may have plagued my family history.

Lord, just as Hannah dedicated Samuel to you, I dedicate my baby to you wholly and completely. Train my ears to hear you and my heart to obey so that I can always be your voice to speak truth and life into his or her life. Train my baby's ears even beyond his or her own years to recognize you and know wisdom. This baby will be kept in safety all the days of his or her life (1 Samuel 25:29). Keep watch over the construction of each nerve, muscle, and canal as it begins to take shape, and strengthen the body's ability to form properly during this critical time.

As my baby's bones begin to develop and harden this week, I reach back into my life and ask that you do inventory. Search my heart, O Lord (Psalm 139:23), for any unforgiveness in my heart and make it plain to me that I might confess and release it, so any root of bitterness can be removed. I refuse to allow this sin that is a thief of peace to pass through another generation and rot the bones of my children and grandchildren (Proverbs 14:30). I speak life and wholeness to any dry bones in my life or generations past (Ezekiel 37:1–14). If there is any feeling of emptiness with unfulfilled dreams and brokenness, I speak healing and life. I listen with open ears and wait for you to show me areas that need to be addressed.

Being Still

Day 1
Meditate on Proverbs 20:12 below. God is literally creating your baby's ears this week. How does that change your perspective of creation itself? God? Your child?

Day 2
What are some practical ways that you could teach your child to hear from God?

Day 3
Ezekiel 37:1–14 talks about a valley of dry bones. Dry bones can be a representation of things lost with no hope of being restored. Ask God to show you one thing that has left you feeling empty without hope of anything changing. Journal what He shows you.

Day 4

Remember your one "dry bone" and imagine that God was sitting in front of it right now. What do you think He would say to it?

Day 5

Go to my website www.iamlelis.com and watch this week's video. God is speaking those words to you. Listen to it a second time, only now imagine that you are speaking those same words to your child. What can you take from this as a prayer for your child every day?

"Ears that hear and eyes that see—the

LORD has made them both."

—Proverbs 20:12 NIV

WEEK 16

*"Children are a heritage from the Lord, offspring
a reward from him. Like arrows in the hands of
a warrior are children born in one's youth"*
—*Psalm 127:3–4*

DID YOU KNOW?

✓ Your baby is the size of an avocado and five inches long.

✓ Your baby is starting to hiccough!

✓ The eyes and ears have landed, and your baby can begin to hear your voice!

✓ The backbone and tiny muscles are getting stronger.

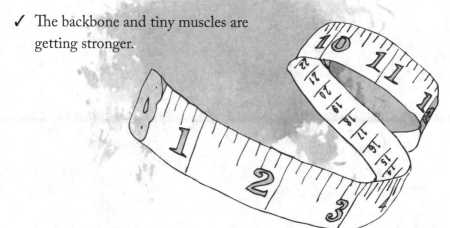

I pray over my baby's back and spine as the tiny muscles begin to gain strength. Father, as those little fingers and hands begin to move around more, searching for things to grasp, use this early stage to begin developing dexterity and coordination. Strengthen the small muscles as my baby reaches in the dark, trying to familiarize him- or herself with the new surroundings. Direct him or her at this early age to reach, grab, pull, stretch, and tug with his or her arms, fingers, and facial muscles. Help this child to begin practicing simple innate functions like making a fist, grabbing the umbilical cord, and sucking his or her thumb. Make my child strong!

Father, my baby's eyes and ears have landed into position! Let those who have eyes let them see and those who can hear let them hear! I speak sight and hearing to my baby's eyes and ears—that they would not only see and hear with clarity in the natural but have a supernatural ability to see you and hear from heaven clearly on a daily basis. Keep my baby from danger by sharpening those senses within him or her (Matthew 13:1–22). I pray that others would be safe around my baby because of the supernatural gifting my precious child has to hear and discern your voice.

Draw back the bow, Father, and aim my baby to the center of the destiny (Psalm 127:5) you have for him or her! Train my heart to follow yours and have a desire to work alongside you to teach my baby about your plans for his or her life so that I can partner with you to ensure he or she is positioned for success. It is your word that says, "You shall also decree a thing, and it shall be established unto thee" (Job 22:28). So I will align my words with that promise and see my child's destiny come to pass.

Being Still

Day 1

Go to my website www.iamlelis.com and watch this week's video. As you listen to the Father's love letter to you, which verse stands out the most? Journal your response back to God about why that is so important to you.

Day 2

Can you think of a time when you didn't seek God for direction on a decision you needed to make? As a small exercise, think of something that you can ask God for direction and journal how He answers?

Day 3

Imagine what your child's life would be like if he or she knew exactly what decisions God wanted him or her to make. Journal a short bedtime prayer the two of you could pray together each night to begin training them to hear God's voice.

Day 4

Your baby can now begin hearing your voice. Why not make up a short silly song to sing over your baby during your bath time? I wonder if he or she will recognize it one day.

Day 5

Very soon you may be finding out the gender of your baby. Have you started thinking about baby names? Jot a few ideas below. I bet your child will find it funny to see what names they could have ended up with!

"And we also thank God continually because, when you received the word of God, which you heard from us, you accepted it not as a human word, but as it actually is, the word of God, which is indeed at work in you who believe."

—1 Thessalonians 2:13 NIV

WEEK 17

"Whether you turn to the right or to the left, your ears will hear a voice behind you, saying, "This is the way; walk in it."

—*Isaiah 30:21*

DID YOU KNOW?

✓ Your baby is the size of the palm of your hand and weighs three and a half ounces.

✓ Your baby's eyes are almost formed and he or she can hear your voice.

✓ One third of your baby's weight is fat.

✓ The heart is regulated by the brain more and becoming less irregular and spontaneous.

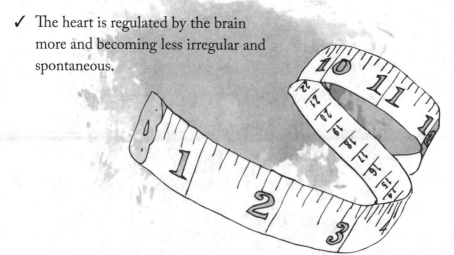

Father, this week my baby's heart is beating stronger and more regularly, thanks to the brain. In the physical realm, put your mighty hands around his or her heart and continue to breathe your *zoë* life into it. In the spiritual realm, send your Holy Spirit to guard it from any offense, so bitterness and unforgiveness will never take root and sacrificial love will always be its motivation.

My baby's ears are also forming this week and he or she is starting to hear and recognize my voice. Father, my heart is to always speak life-giving words to this precious one, so I ask that you reveal any unforgiveness in my life that would cause me to withhold love from him or her.

Let me not become so familiar with the natural progression of pregnancy that I forget this is a supernatural miracle taking place inside my womb (Matthew 13:13–16). Lord, it brings me to tears to know that my baby did not have the ability to hear a week ago, but this week my baby does, and the first voice my baby will ever hear will be mine! It's humbling when I think that the power of my words these next few months will be what will shape and create the atmosphere in which my baby will grow and develop. Guard my heart so that every word I speak will glorify you and bring fruit to my womb (Proverbs 4:22–24).

As healthy fat begins forming around my baby's bones and protecting his or her internal organs this week, I am thankful that it is your way to cushion, nourish, and protect his or her five-inch, petite frame. Lord, everything you're doing is a gift and a blessing for my baby, and I rest in peace and confidence that you are directing my thoughts.

Being Still

Day 1

Thumb through the book of Proverbs and find five "power" words that best describe how God sees us as his sons and daughters. For instance, He sees us as courageous, lovely, fearless and so forth. Write a fun short poem that you could sing over your baby daily, so your baby will always hear how God sees them.

Day 2

Read Psalm 139:23. Ask the Holy Spirit to search your heart and show you anything that He would like to rid you of today. Journal your thoughts.

Day 3

Have your started feeling your baby move yet? When do you notice it most?

Day 4

How have you been handling the change in hormones and anxiety level of things to come?

Day 5

Now that your belly is growing and baby is more noticeable,
how do you feel about complete strangers walking up to you
and touching your belly?

What old-wives' tales have you heard that gives you an

indication of whether you are having a boy or a girl?

WEEK 18

"I will teach all your children, and they will enjoy great peace. You will be secure under a government that is just and fair. Your enemies will stay far away. You will live in peace, and terror will not come near. If any nation comes to fight you, it is not because I sent them. Whoever attacks you will go down in defeat."
—Isaiah 54:13–15

DID YOU KNOW?

✓ Your baby is the size of a sweet potato and is five inches long.

✓ Myelin is insulating nerves that help your baby get stronger.

✓ You will start to feel your baby move around more.

✓ A girl will have her fallopian tubes and uterus in place, and a boy's prostate will start to form.

✓ The five senses are beginning to become more alert.

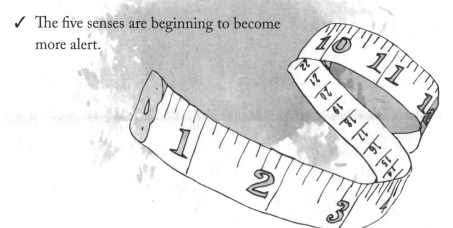

Isaiah 54:13–15: oh how I love this scripture! It reminds me that you don't send trouble my way to teach me a lesson, but if trouble does come, I will remain in peace in the midst of it because I will not be defeated. Father, show me how I can pass that confidence on to my children, so when the enemy stands before them with accusations and lies, they will not agree with it, but instead shut the mouth of the enemy and believe your truth about them. Show me ways to speak your truth about my baby's present and future so that truth will be hidden inside them (Psalm 119:11) and others will be safe in their presence.

I trust you will watch over my baby both today and in years to come so that others will be protected by the confidence and intimate relationship he or she has in you. I trust you will show me what and how to pray (Jeremiah 33:3) as each season of his or her life unfolds.

Father I pray for my baby's brain, spinal cord, and nerve endings and command that the white corpuscles and healthy nerves begin to line up and communicate quickly and accurately the way you've designed them to work. You said that "as a man thinks in his heart, so is he" (Proverbs 23:7), so, Holy Spirit, I ask you to begin training me to think on things that are true, noble, right, pure, lovely, and admirable—all that is excellent (Philippians 4:8)! Discipline me so that as a parent I can pass that fruit as an example to my child.

Cover my baby's mind and entire nervous system during this time of growth, and cancel any generational sin or destructive thought patterns that are opposite the mind of Christ that could bring damage or rejection into his or her life.

Being Still

Day 1

Myelin is an insulation around your baby's nerves that is helping him or her with stronger movements. Are there times that you can feel your baby more than others? Have you noticed certain foods trigger this?

Day 2

Taste, sight, smell, touch, and hearing are the five senses that are becoming more developed in your baby this week. Can you find scripture verses that relate to each of these senses and incorporate it into a prayer?

Day 3

Your baby is beginning to recognize and respond to your voice, in particular. How does that make you feel?

Day 4

The opening scripture for this week says "I will teach your children and they will have great peace." In what ways could you create an intimate time of prayer and worship that would reinforce the peace of God and act like a seed being sown generationally into your developing baby?

Day 5

Find a quiet, soothing song this week that you can hum to your baby—can you begin to notice that he or she responds to your voice?

... then sings my soul.

—Carl Boberg, "How Great Thou Art"

WEEK 19

*"That he might sanctify and cleanse it with
the washing of water by the word,"*

—*Ephesians 5:26*

DID YOU KNOW?

✓ Your baby is the size of a large mango and is one-half pound and six inches long.

✓ Your baby's skin has a protective coating called vermix.

✓ More brown fat is developing to maintain regular body temperature.

✓ Your little girl now has 6 million eggs in her ovaries.

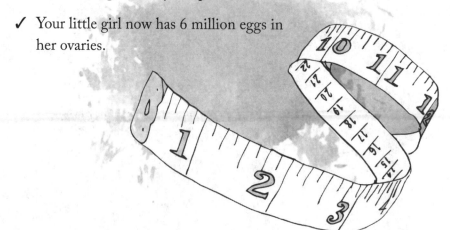

[Prayer for girl]

Lord I pray for my baby and thank you that before my baby is even born you are already preparing for the next generation—my grandchildren! At only nineteen weeks, you have already developed inside my precious daughter's six-inch frame six million eggs! What a generational God! Father, I cover her delicate body with purity and ask that you sanctify her so that she is hidden from the hand of the enemy. Protect what she hears and what she sees so that she is never disillusioned by the enemy about her identity as being a "daughter" of the Most High in heaven.

I pray over the five senses of the body that are beginning to develop stronger this week. As the neurons are beginning to send more messages from the brain to the muscles, my baby will have the ability to kick stronger and more often. Father I pray over all parts of the brain that are sending messages throughout the body and command that it would fire signals throughout the body accurately so that each limb can react and respond accordingly. I stand in the gap of any strokes or brain trauma that may have occurred in our family blood line that could prevent proper growth or lay dormant and cause paralysis later in life. I speak peace and order over his or her complete development.

It has already been determined if my child will be a right-brain or a left-brain thinker—creative or technical. Regardless of how you created him or her, it is in a unique way, and I commit to champion those gifts, never comparing to others. I come into covenant with you to speak and think according to your word and principles, reminding my baby that you, above all else, have given us the mind of Christ (1 Corinthians 2:16), so however my baby thinks—it was by your design!

Being Still

Day 1

Go to my website www.iamlelis.com and watch this week's video. Meditate on what Dr. Leaf taught about our thoughts. What have you been thinking about lately?

Day 2

Do you allow your mind to think on nothing or something? Is the something that you think about a destructive thought or a life-giving thought that agrees with how God created you to think?

Day 3

Do you think that you can live a life of *not* disciplining your mind (what you think about daily) and still walk in the purposes of God? What can you do to create the proper building blocks in your child as the brain is being developed?

Day 4

What "toxic trees" can you identify in your life that have stemmed from memories of your past? What might you do and say to uproot those toxic trees and plant "green Christmas trees" so as to build a healthy thought.

Day 5

Write a short dialogue that you can speak over your life as well as your baby so that together, "healthy trees" can begin to grow and develop.

Did you know that your baby has begun practicing sucking his or her thumb?

WEEK 20

"He will cover you with His feathers, And under His wings you will find refuge; His faithfulness will be your shield and rampart. You will not fear the terror of night, nor of the arrow that flies by day "

—Psalm 91:4–5

DID YOU KNOW?

✓ Your baby is the size of a small cantaloupe.

✓ Your baby will begin to suck its thumb and pull on the umbilical cord.

✓ Your little girl's uterus is fully formed, and her vaginal canal is developing.

✓ Your little boy's testicles are descending from the abdomen to the scrotum.

Lord, we are halfway home! Hallelujah! This week my baby's brown fat cells are arriving on the scene and multiplying at a rapid pace to keep his or her internal organs warm until birth. Just as you cover us with the shadow of your wings and protect us from anything that would try to harm us, the brown fat cells are covering and protecting my baby's organs (Psalms 91:4).

> This week my baby girl has a fully-formed uterus, and her ovaries have millions of eggs ready for her to begin her own family one day. If there is anything that would prevent my little girl from becoming pregnant, I pray and command right now, in Jesus Name that those things would reverse and align. I cover her and pray into generations to come and declare that together she and I will leave a legacy of hope and peace that our grandchildren and great-grandchildren will one day walk in.

> This week my son's testicles are formed in the abdomen, and I pray that he would grow into a strong, fruitful man with the desire to have a family of his own one day. I pray over my little boy that he would know you all the days of his life and have a heart to leave a legacy of spiritual fathers in his own offspring for generations to come.

Father, I pray that my baby will grow to know and love you all the days of their life and have a family of their own one day to teach of the faithfulness you showed in their lives (Judges 2:8–10). The atmosphere of my home will always display how loving and faithful you have been in our lives (Psalm 145:4). Father, I pray that my legacy of prayer over my baby will be passed down to my grandchildren so that as a family—generationally—we will continue to give you the glory (Deuteronomy 6:7) and walk in your blessings as a result of it!

Being Still

Day 1
Read this week's verse below. What would you say was a "mighty act of God," and why do you think it's important as parents to teach your children about them?

Day 2
Did you grow up in a home where God's faithfulness of answered prayers were openly discussed, or was God only mentioned on Sunday or not at all? Journal how you would like to continue or change. Why?

Day 3
How do you think your decisions in life would have been different if you'd lived in a home where God's faithfulness was always spoken or not spoken?

Day 4
What are a few creative ways that you could think of to incorporate everyday things into a teaching moment of answered prayers to your children?

Day 5
Spend some time writing the entire Psalm 145. Ask the Holy Spirit to illuminate any verse that God would want you to stop and meditate over. Journal your thoughts, so you can remember God's faithfulness and share them with your child one day.

"One generation commends your works to another; they tell of your mighty acts.

—Psalm 145:4 NIV

WEEK 21

*"... to make her holy, cleansing her by the
washing with water through the word, "*

—*Ephesians 5:26*

DID YOU KNOW?

✓ Your baby is the size of a large carrot.

✓ Small amounts of sugar are beginning to
filter into the amniotic fluid.

✓ Your baby's bone marrow is now
developed and is helping the liver and
spleen to produce blood cells.

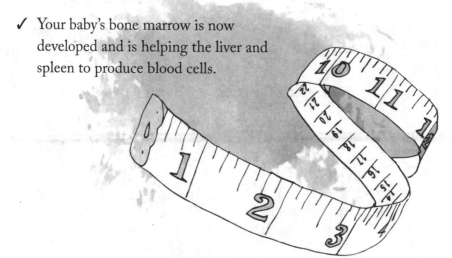

This week, my baby's liver and spleen are growing and will work continually to keep his or her body clean from impurities. Just as these organs rid the body of harmful toxins, maturing in your word will rid our lives of toxic relationships and make us wise to the traps and lies of the enemy. I pray that this baby would use the word as a sword against the lies of the world and would always be a truth bearer—holy and sanctified in your eyes—a light in a dark world so others would come to know you through his or her godly character.

I also lift up my baby's red blood cells, platelets, and white blood cells that are multiplying within the bone marrow this week. As a soldier fighting off his enemy, I pray the cell walls would be strong and undivided. Just as a champion fighter takes down his opponent, his or her white blood cells would always be ready to stop any virus or illness (2 Samuel 17:10) at its onset. I pray my baby's heart would always be softened to desire you, and any spiritual assault that would try to leave the debris of unforgiveness or bitterness would find no ground to take root and cause physical illness.

I pray also for the sugar that my baby is beginning to take in through my diet so that he or she can stay nourished and hydrated. I commit to watching the food I eat, so my baby can grow healthy and not lack the necessary nutrients required for their growing little body. I come against any past family history of diabetes in my family line and bind any rejection, self-hatred, guilt, or abuse that can develop into this disease, if not addressed. By the authority you have given me as a believer and spiritual covering for my child, I pray in the name of Jesus that all physical manifestation from the spiritual tentacles of this extreme rejection be canceled.

Father, you are a good and loving Father, and I thank you that you are setting things in perfect order for future generations.

Being Still

Day 1

Have you found out if you are going to have a baby boy or baby girl? Journal your emotions the moment you found out.

Day 2

What unusual things have you been experiencing this week of your pregnancy?

Day 3

Knowing that your baby will be taking in the sugar content of what your body is processing this week, what healthy choices have you made in your diet that will help promote a healthy baby during pregnancy?

Day 4
Read the verse below. What do you think God was talking about when He spoke of a "heart of stone" and a "heart of flesh"?

Day 5
Stretch marks. Okay, yes, I said it—ugh. What have you found to help prevent or get rid of them?

"I will give them an undivided heart and put a new spirit in them; I will remove from them their heart of stone and give them a heart of flesh."

—Ezekiel 11:19

WEEK 22

"For we are God's handiwork, created in Christ Jesus to do good works, which God prepared in advance for us to do."

—*Ephesians 2:10*

DID YOU KNOW?

✓ Your baby is the size of a small doll.

✓ Your baby's eyes are still sealed shut but can still detect light, and the ears can hear and process sounds.

✓ The nervous system is getting stronger and more sensitive.

✓ Your baby is learning to use its fingers to grab for their ears, nose, and toes.

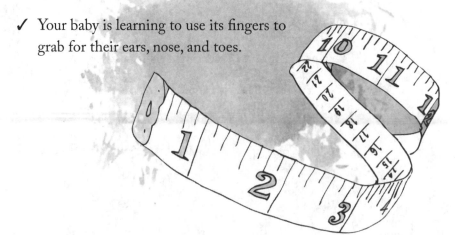

Even though my baby's eyes are still sealed shut, my baby can still move them around side to side and recognize light when it shines on my belly. Father, I lift up the optic nerves that connect the eye to the brain and speak strength and precision, so potential obstructions will never prevent images from being transmitted to the brain. Just as you sharpen those physical eyes, I pray that his or her spiritual eyes would always see you working behind the scenes, even when you show no evidence of it around him or her. Proverbs 13:12 says that *"Hope deferred makes the heart sick but a longing fulfilled is the tree of life."* Father, I ask that the intimacy of your relationship with my baby manifest itself through the confidence and strength my baby would display during the dark and quiet times and that he or she would never to be tempted to surrender to despair and discouragement when your promises are delayed from his or her timetable.

I lift up my baby's ears to you also and pray that even in the distractions and chaos of the world, this child would recognize and obey your voice at a young age (1 Samuel 3). Father, your love is precious and unfailing; I pray my baby would trust you always to stay in the shadow of your wings (Psalm 36:7), never desiring to follow a pattern written by the world. I pray that the bones in his or her ears would form precisely as you've created them so that infections would not develop and lead to problems requiring surgery for a ventilation tube during the childhood years. I speak to the ear growth and say that they will form the way you have designed them to work, and no complications will arise. Those who have ears to hear let them hear (Matthew 11:15)!

Being Still

Day 1

Are you planning to find out the sex of your baby? If you have already found out, how are you (and your immediate family) feeling about this new discovery?

Day 2

Have you started feeling your feet begin to swell? Some moms even experience an increase in shoe size. Compare this week to past pregnancies or even before you were pregnant.

Day 3

Has your baby begun to kick more this week? Have you noticed your baby kicking more for one person than the other? Any funny stories?

Day 4

Has your growing belly started interrupting your sleep each night? What creative things have you discovered to help with encouraging your sleep?

Day 5

Hormones, leg cramps, nesting, belly buttons! What off-the-wall things have you been experiencing this week that have forced you to adapt to this little baby growing in your belly?

JESUS LOVES ME

Jesus loves me, this I know,
for the Bible tells me so.
Little ones to Him belong;
they are weak, but He is strong.

Refrain:
Yes, Jesus loves me! Yes, Jesus loves me!
Yes, Jesus loves me! The Bible tells me so.

—Anna Bartlett Warner (1859)

WEEK 23

"The Spirit of God has made me, And the breath of the Almighty gives me life"

—*Job 33:4*

DID YOU KNOW?

✓ Your baby is the size of a papaya.

✓ The lung cells are forming and maturing, preparing to breathe.

✓ Small capillaries are forming in the lungs and preparing to expand after birth.

✓ The placenta is transferring oxygen and nutrients to your baby and removing waste.

Lord, I speak health over my body, and I know that I lack no good thing because you are supplying my every need both physically and spiritually (Philippians 4:19). As a sifter removes unwanted particles from the flour, that is a prophetic picture of what your hands do for my life. "No good thing do you withhold from those whose walk is upright" (Psalm 84:11). We'll never know the things you've rescued us from when we put our trust in you. So, Father, use your hands as a filter over my life, body, and baby that I am carrying and remove all toxins from my body physically, spiritually, or generationally.

Cleanse my body, so as oxygen and nutrients from my body transfer to the placenta through the umbilical cord, only healthy nutrients will be delivered into my baby's growing and developing body. As a deer pants for water (Psalm 42:1), create in me a desire for water, healthy food, exercise, restful sleep, and your presence. Strengthen my body to carry a healthy baby, so my baby can reap the benefits with healthy cells filled with oxygen that can nurture his or her small, growing body.

Father, just as you created me, you are creating my baby (Genesis 1:27), and just as you breathed life into Adam's lungs (Genesis 2:7), you are also breathing life into my baby's lungs this week. Before my little one takes their first breath outside the womb, I know they will have been first filled with your mighty breath, so I pray those lungs will always be strong and airways open.

Lord, you watch over the things that concern us (Psalm 138:8), and I rest in knowing that you are watching over my baby. Add keratin to his or her body so that their skin will thicken and have the ability to grow as the bones grow even after my baby is born.

Being Still

Day 1

Have you planned for your maternity leave, and when you plan on returning to work?

Day 2

Go to my website www.iamlelis.com and watch this week's video. How does your "baby bump" compare to the bellies you noticed on the other moms? Have strangers started touching your belly randomly? How do you react to this?

Day 3

This week we are praying over your pancreas and how its physical function relates to a spiritual picture of God filtering and removing toxic lies that can affect you physically and unknowingly pass down generationally. Get quiet with God and ask Him to show you the lie that you've carried and agreed with unknowingly. Acknowledge it then repent and journal that lie.

Day 4
Ask God to replace the lie you journaled about yesterday with the truth that He says about you. What is He saying to you?

Day 5
In this week's video, what is your good, bad, and ugly moments during this week of your pregnancy?

"You are my hiding place and my shield: I hope in your word."

—Psalm 119:114 KJV

WEEK 24

"Indeed, the very hairs of your head are all numbered. Don't be afraid; you are worth more than many sparrows."

—Luke 12:7

DID YOU KNOW?

✓ Your baby is the size of an ear of corn.

✓ Your baby is starting to form eyebrows, eyelashes and hair.

✓ More muscles are beginning to form.

✓ Your baby is hearing and recognizing sounds more often, even songs.

✓ If born prematurely, your baby can survive out of the womb.

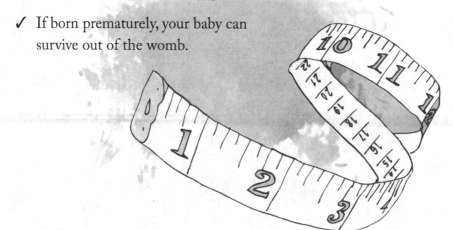

I'm thinking of the careful attention a seamstress gives to threading a needle. One hand waits patiently, and the other moves forward steadily as the watchful eye focuses on the placement of the thread. The two will soon come together as a useful instrument to begin the task of either mending or creating. Oh, how that is the picture of you and me, Father. I wait. You move. The Holy Spirit guides. You are so intimate with every detail of my life.

As my baby's hair begins to grow, I have this image of you lying on your side, smiling and singing as you count each hair that will soon sprout from that small head. You loved me first, and you adore me (Zephaniah 3:17). Before I was created in my mother's womb, before I was born, and even in my sin, you first loved me, and that makes me fall in love (Romans 2:4) with you all the more. I want to show that same love to my baby and teach him or her of your patient heart.

I have this image of the potter and his clay. His skillful hand takes pleasure in each detail that he purposely marks as his own (Isaiah 45:9). As you begin molding my baby's facial features this week, I know that my baby will look just as you purposed him or her to look. I pray that my baby will embrace their identity in you and not in the value of their appearance. I pray that my baby would have a God-confidence and never be tricked into comparing him or herself to the world's standards, and their beauty would be as a result of the time he or she spends in your presence (Exodus 34:29).

I lift up the recall memory in the brain and pray that my baby would begin to develop and recognize my voice as I sing and speak to him or her. Father, strengthen this baby's growing muscles inside his one and one-half–pound body and all the developing organs, so they would all work in concert together, functioning the way you designed them to be.

Being Still

Day 1

Go to my website www.iamlelis.com and watch this week's video. As you focus on the words of the song below what "tender whispers" have you heard in your dark days that tell you God loves you and is pleased with you? If you've never heard it, journal how that makes you feel and ask Him to open up your ears to hear and recognize Him.

Day 2

In week 4, we committed to exercising during your pregnancy. What have you dedicated yourself to, and how has that contributed to your sleeping patterns and healthy eating habits? If you aren't exercising, journal what is holding you back, and commit to a routine today.

Day 3

Have you been able to spend quiet time alone with just you and God during your pregnancy? What nuggets have you taken away thus far that reinforces how He is in the details of your life and is well pleased with you?

Day 4

Have you noticed changes in your body this week, like dry-ness of skin, swelling, headaches, or constipation? What other things have you noticed either in your body or with your crav-ings or food intake?

Day 5

Have you found a special friend who is also pregnant during this short season? Journal how this has helped or ask God to join you to someone special.

Good Good Father

I've heard a thousand stories of what they think you're like,

But I've heard the tender whispers of love in the dead of night,

And you tell me that you're pleased,

And that I'm never alone

You're a good, good Father

It's who you are, it's who you are, it's who you are.

—Chris Tomlin

WEEK 25

"When Elizabeth heard Mary's greeting, the baby leaped in her womb, and Elizabeth was filled with the Holy Spirit."
—*Luke 1:41*

DID YOU KNOW?

✓ Your baby is the size of a cauliflower and is thirteen inches tall.

✓ Your baby may respond to your voice or noises with a kick, as startle reflexes are developing.

✓ The nostrils are starting to open and beginning to practice breathing with amniotic fluid.

✓ Blood vessels are developing in the lungs.

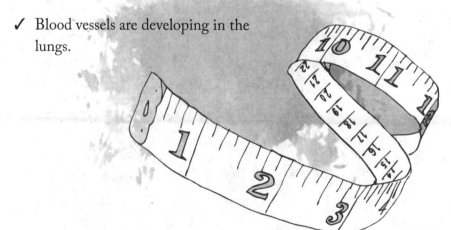

The moment Elizabeth saw Mary and heard her voice, the baby leaped in her womb (Luke 1:41). Father, this week as my baby's startle reflexes strengthen and my baby responds immediately to our voices with stronger kicks, I decree that his or her heart would react with the same joy when my baby hears your voice speak, even when it's a whisper. What a sweet, intimate picture of what the word of God does in our lives as it awakens things inside us and consequently causes us to behave differently.

John 1:1 says that "In the beginning was the Word and the Word was with God and the Word was God." John 1:14 says "The Word became flesh and made his dwelling among us. We have seen his glory, the glory of the one and only Son, who came from the Father, full of grace and truth."

I believe that as I become filled with the Spirit and speak your word that it will not return void but create an atmosphere for my baby to grow healthy and into your purposes (Isaiah 55:11). I pray that he or she will always have a heart that is moldable and pliable for your word, and in each transitional season of life, my child will be drawn to natural mentors just as Mary was to Elizabeth, Elisha was to Elijah, and Timothy was to Paul.

Father, as my baby's nostrils begin to open up this week and the lungs begin to develop more, I ask that you breathe your *zoë* life into him or her just as you did for Adam. Let my baby's countenance always reflect the peace that they have in their heart, trusting in you to keep your promises. Anxiety has no place, sickness has no place, and disease has no place. My baby would be a truth-bearer and carry your hope inside so that others would be encouraged in their season of despair.

Being Still

Day 1

Go to my website www.iamlelis.com and watch this week's video. This is an amazing picture of a child recognizing the voice of her natural father. Can you describe a time your heavenly Father comforted you? If not, quiet your heart and ask Him to show you that moment when you thought you were alone but He was there. Journal your time with Him now.

Day 2

Reflecting on this week's video, what routine have you developed with your baby to reinforce that they will recognize and possibly respond to your voice once they are born?

Day 3

Read Luke 1:5–17. This prophetic message came days before Zechariah and his wife were pregnant and at an age where they were "old and advanced in years." Why do you think God chose this couple instead of a young couple that was fertile or had a home filled with children?

Day 4

What seven things did the messenger angel Gabriel prophecy to Zechariah the priest about his unborn son?

Day 5

Do an inventory of your life and family. Do you think God might have at least one prophetic message for your child to walk into? Pray and ask God to speak to you about it. Journal your time with God.

"We see patterns that repeat from mothers and fathers to their children. This is true in both biological and spiritual disease. Exodus 20 teaches about the sins of the father being passed on to the third and fourth generation."

—*Dr. Henry Wright*

WEEK 26

"Set your minds on things above, not on earthly things."
—*Colossians 3:2*

DID YOU KNOW?

✓ Your baby is the size of a chuck roast.

✓ Your baby's eyes are now open and are responding to light.

✓ Brain waves are getting stronger and becoming more active.

✓ As your baby starts swallowing amniotic fluid, the lungs are developing as they practice.

"Set your minds." Immediately I got a picture of a toy train being locked in and "set" on its tracks. A train is not supposed to function like a car on the road. A train can only operate the way it was designed—on a track. Our minds are designed by you, Lord, to function only on the things above, *the word of God*—not on the earthly things that are *circumstances around us.*

This week, my baby's brain waves are becoming stronger and more active, sending millions of messages simultaneously throughout the body. I declare a sharp mind that is quick to learn and comprehend. I come against confusion and wrong thinking that doesn't line up with your truth. My baby will be a child that will have a habit of rightly dividing the word of God (2 Timothy 2:15) for themselves and others, so they will never fall into the trap of lies set by the enemy, twisting good intentions into destructive arrows.

As my baby's brain activity gets stronger, I ask that you would be a guard over it, so he or she would have the ability to think and retain information far beyond the years appointed to them.

Father, let my baby's eyes be as sharp in the spiritual as they are in the natural; let them always seek You and righteousness, and let their ears be attentive to You like a sheep who knows the voice of his or her shepherd (John 10:27). Just as you fill his or her lungs with air and breathe into them, I declare that my baby would always be a person who breathes life into others, always edifying and always speaking truth (Ephesians 4:29).

Being Still

Day 1

At twenty-six weeks, you would think that your hormones would have subsided even if just a little by now. What things have you noticed about either your body or your emotions that are a result of your ever-changing body?

Day 2

With all this moving going around in your belly, have you noticed any visible body parts poking out your belly?

Day 3

What are some of the things you've considered with regard to your location and methods of birth?

Day 4
If this is not your first child, have you noticed your belly larger
or smaller than previous pregnancies? Do you feel you should
be larger or smaller in size than you already are?

Day 5
What unusual food cravings have you noticed yourself starting
to have?

A lot of parents choose a name for their children

before they are born. Have you considered asking

the Lord what name He has for your child?

WEEK 27

"But they will never follow a stranger; in fact, they will run away from him because they do not recognize a stranger's voice . . . My sheep listen to my voice; I know them, and they follow me."
—John 10:5, 27

DID YOU KNOW?

✓ Your baby is the size of a rutabaga.

✓ Your baby's taste buds are beginning to develop.

✓ The lungs are developing, and at times, you will feel your baby's hiccoughs increase.

✓ If you press your hand to your belly, you will feel your baby's heartbeat stronger.

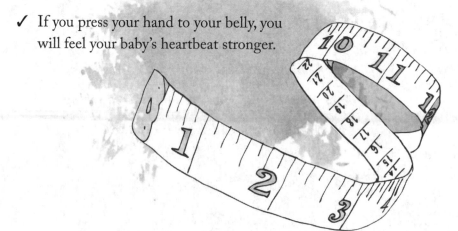

This week, my baby's ears are hearing things more clearly, and I'm amazed that when I speak, pray, or sing over him or her, though muffled in my belly, my child can hear. I'm confident that once he is born, my baby will recognize my voice and respond, knowing that I can be trusted to protect him or her. Father, as I study your word and meditate on your promises, give me an instructed tongue to know the word that sustains the weary. As I speak life to others, let my words be seeds planted into my baby's heart so that when he or she awakens morning by morning, he or she would awaken with ears to hear like one being taught (Isaiah 50:4). Let my baby use your word like a sword (Hebrews 4:12) to cast down every thought or vain imagination (2 Corinthians 10:5) and shut the mouth of the lion (Daniel 6:22) that would try to roar in his ears to take them off the straight path you have for them (Isaiah 45:2).

Father, your word says that we should taste and see that you are good (Psalm 34:8) and to be salt and light (Matthew 5:13) to a world that desperately needs you. Just as salt enhances and supports the flavor of the food, my baby's relationship with you will be so genuine and intimate that others would sense chains and walls falling in their lives when in his or her presence.

I pray over my baby's taste buds as they are getting instructions this week! They will be able to taste everything I eat a few hours later. Father develop those small tiny hairs on my baby's tongue and fine-tune the brain signals to distinguish sweet, sour, bitter, or salty. Let my child grow into a person whose words would be life-giving and fruitful to those that would hear it.

Being Still

Day 1
Has your baby started experiencing hiccoughs yet? Describe a few of the instances where you've noticed your belly moving. Is it typically done after certain foods or times of the day?

Day 2
How is your exercise regimen going these days? Are you finding it harder to do with your baby bump?

Day 3
Are there currently other siblings in your home? How have you begun preparing them for the little baby brother or sister in your belly?

Day 4

The Bible shows us that God had a purpose in advance for Jeremiah, Jesus, and John the Baptist. Since He is no respecter of persons, what could you imagine He had planned for you before you were born?

Day 5

Have you noticed your body swelling in your feet or hands or pressure in unusual places other than your belly?

You are clothed in strength and dignity.

—Proverbs 31

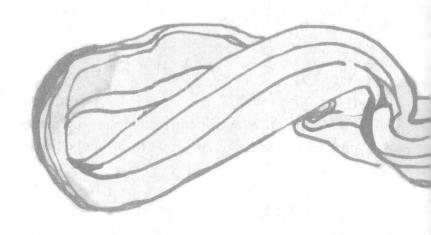

THIRD TRIMESTER
WEEK 28–40

"You will also decree a thing, and it will be established for you; and light will shine on your ways."

—Job 22:28

WEEK 28

"Yes, you have been with me from birth; from my mother's womb you have cared for me. No wonder I am always praising you!"
—*Psalm 71:6*

DID YOU KNOW?

✓ Your baby is the size of an eggplant.

✓ Your baby is experiencing REM sleep. and it appears like they are dreaming.

✓ Your baby is beginning to stick its tongue out and taste the amniotic fluid.

✓ The lungs are stronger now and allowing more breathing, sucking, and coughing.

Psalm 71:6: oh how I love that verse! Father, with all that I've gone through in my life, I've done it too often without you. How that must have hurt to see me turn my back from you, refusing help. Lord, I will no longer do things outside of you; I lay everything down at your feet. Help me to raise my baby to praise you through both the good and the bad seasons of life.

This week, my baby begins to have dreams and will begin to practice opening and closing their eyes. Father, your heart's desire has always been to speak to us, and one way is through dreams and visions (Acts 2:17). Your word says that those who know you also have the ability to interpret and discern what you are saying to us. Thank you for this gift (Ephesians 4:11), and I pray that my baby will honor you with learning how to interpret those dreams and visions (Revelation 2:29) and change the world around them as a result of it.

I decree that sweet precious child, doors will be opened on your behalf, and it will be as though God himself were standing in your presence telling you of things to come (Revelation 4:1). God will entrust you with his assignment, given through dreams and visions, because you will carry them out with great passion.

You will walk in confidence and will not back down from any attack the enemy might bring to frighten you in the form of nightmares or night terrors.

Your faith and trust in God to keep his word (Jeremiah 1:12) will allow you to supernaturally pull down strongholds (2 Corinthians 10:4), create order, and establish peace that others will be drawn to. You will walk in your destiny and take dominion over every area your foot treads, closing all doors from past generations that may try to gain a foothold to your life and future generations.

Being Still

Day 1
Reflecting for a moment that your baby is beginning to experience dreams in your womb, have you noticed an increase of dreams yourself?

Day 2
What dreams did you have for yourself as a young girl, if any?

Day 3
Even though the purposes for our lives come from God, how would you like to prepare your child to hear and walk in the dreams God has for him or her?

Day 4

Your body is working harder now because of everything going on inside your belly. How have you been sneaking in cat naps to allow your body to rest?

Day 5

How has your "bump" changed this pregnancy compared to your previous ones or other pregnant moms around you?

"At Gibeon the Lord appeared to Solomon during the night in a dream, and God said, 'Ask for whatever you want me to give you.'"

—*1 Kings 3:5*

WEEK 29

*"I sought the Lord, and he answered me; he delivered
me from all my fears. Those who look to him are radiant;
their faces are never covered with shame."*

—*Psalm 34:4–5*

DID YOU KNOW?

✓ Your baby is the size of an acorn squash
and is sixteen inches long weighing
two-and-a-half pounds.

✓ Buds of permanent teeth are forming
under the gums.

✓ The adrenal glands are producing
hormones.

✓ White fat is forming to provide energy
and healthy weight for your baby.

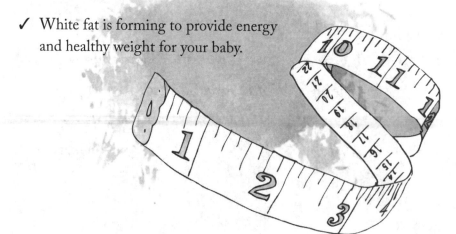

Father, even in the little things, you have a purpose. As white fat cells begin developing this week, they have a different purpose from the brown fat cells that began developing in week 19. While white fat cells are there to produce energy, warmth, and cushion our internal organs, brown fat cells are there to burn calories in order to generate heat for the body. I pray for a lifestyle of healthy living and healthy eating, so my baby has the correct proportion of brown fat cells needed to burn unnecessary calories.

I lift up the buds of teeth that you are dropping in their proper place this week and pray that no permanent teeth will be missing, that they will *all* be strong, and my baby will have *no* future problems with his or her jaw or abnormal growth in his or her teeth. Lord, I lift up my own body as my adrenal glands begin to produce additional hormones and estrogen to stimulate my milk production. Surround me with patient, godly women so when my emotions run high and I'm a little unreasonable because of all the changes inside my body, they can speak love and truth and I will have a heart to receive it.

I decree that sweet little one, you will never allow the enemy to bring fear or shame on you because your appearance may be different than the way the world views as normal —you are healthy, you are chosen, and God has created you to stand out (1 Peter 2:9)! You will have a guard around what you hear, and your voice will break any lie spoken over you. Others will be safe in your presence because you will never fear to speak truth and justice over any lie that is contrary to the word of God.

Good things are stored up inside you because of the Holy Spirit (Matthew 12:35). Your patience will never run thin, and you will never become overwhelmed. You will create a peaceful atmosphere, and people will be drawn to you because you will be quick to listen and slow to speak (James 1:19) and will always be full of wisdom to speak truth.

Being Still

Day 1

This week's scripture says that "I sought the Lord and he answered, he delivered me from my fears." If you were honest about what has been one of your biggest fears that you can't seem to shake, how could you allow God to give you peace?

Day 2

As you round the corner in your third trimester, have you noticed yourself nesting more? How have you started preparing for your new arrival?

Day 3

So, we've talked about exercise and eating healthy during your pregnancy. How have you been doing these last few weeks? What can you do to incorporate a small exercise program into your busy schedule?

Day 4

How do you feel different, entering your third trimester as opposed to your second?

Day 5

It's common at this point of your pregnancy for your belly to start feeling tighter, and you feel pressure. When do you notice this happening more—early morning? After eating particular foods?

"When I fall to my knees you're the one who pulls me up again."

—"You Don't Miss a Thing"

Bethel Music

WEEK 30

"Shout for joy to the LORD, all the earth,
burst into jubilant song with music;"

—*Psalm 98:4*

DID YOU KNOW?

✓ Your baby is the size of a napa cabbage.

✓ The brain is getting bigger and forming
grooves and indentions in preparation
for more tissue to form.

✓ The bone marrow has now completely
taken over production of making red
blood cells.

✓ Your baby's hands are formed.

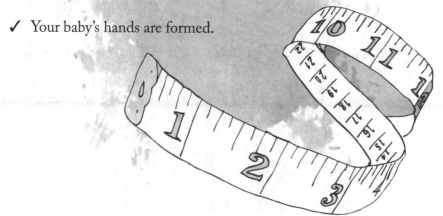

This week as my baby's brain begins to develop and the surface becomes more wrinkled with indentions to allow for more brain tissue and growth, I pray that the capacity to learn would be increased and any previous history of brain trauma or predisposition to potential strokes that may create a risk in the brain be removed in Jesus' name.

Train me as well, Father, to only speak life-giving words that would encourage and uplift my little one. Give me patience to know his or her heart and wisdom to see that each child should be parented differently. Show me how to instruct without breaking his or her spirit (Ephesians 6:4). Break any lies that I've believed about myself (Proverbs 14:30) or what any other family members have wrestled with, and help me to resist giving in to defeat that my baby will follow in family sin patterns.

I pray that the bone marrow begins to multiply healthy red blood cells for the hemoglobin to carry oxygen to all the organs and tissues in the body. Lord, allow my baby to deliver full term and not come early. Allow his or her red blood cells to increase in the proper amount of iron, folate, vitamin E, and other nutrients so that infection does not set in and my baby is not born with anemia and does not develop jaundice after birth.

Dear Baby, you are a person whose thoughts are covered with the blood of Christ. You guard your mind and never allow it to wander into negative, corrupt or destructive thinking. You will stay on the straight path that God has purposed for you to walk. My baby, you will have a merry, sound and thankful heart, and it will be life to your flesh. You will never allow envy or jealousy to enter your heart (Proverbs 17:22) because you know it dries the bones. You were not created to suffer but to prosper and be in good health (3 John 1:2).

Being Still

Day 1
Some moms have decided to have a belly cast before they deliver for a keepsake. What are your thoughts on doing this for yourself?

Day 2
Assuming you've already chosen a name for your sweet baby, what is the meaning of the name you chose or are considering?

Day 3
We're praying over the brain and the mind this week. Have you ever made the distinction between the two?

Day 4
Could you say that you have the mind of Christ, or do you allow your thoughts to rob you of peace? Journal that inner dialogue, then listen to what God would say about that same thing.

Day 5
Do you notice that you struggle with some of the same lies that your mother or father wrestle(d) with? What could you do to prevent that from continuing in your life and it being a stronghold in your child's life?

"The Lord did for Sarah what he had promised ...
Abraham gave the name Isaac to the son Sarah bore
him ... Sarah said, 'God has brought me laughter.'"
—Genesis 21:1-6

WEEK 31

*"May my prayer be set before you like incense; may the
lifting up of my hands be like the evening sacrifice."*

—*Psalm 141:2*

DID YOU KNOW?

✓ Your baby is the size of a pineapple,
sixteen inches long and three pounds.

✓ Your baby can now turn its head side to
side.

✓ The brain is processing signals, the nose
is ready to smell, and the heartbeat
races and slows down as things are
recognized.

✓ Your baby is urinating two cups of liquid
a day.

✓ Babies are born with about 10,000 taste
buds.

Taste, hear, touch, smell, sight—all systems are go, and all five senses are fully functional! My baby's nose is fine-tuned through the smells emanating through the amniotic fluid, and the growing number of taste buds are distinguishing which foods are preferred over others. Father, I am aware that my baby can hear me clearly when I speak and can respond to music very easily, so keep me aware of the things I say and listen to during this time in my life. Use the moments when lights shine on my belly to sharpen the muscles in their eyes. Fine tune all the senses, Father, so the central nervous system can learn to receive it, organize it, and determine the correct response.

I lift up the development of the kidneys and urinary tract this week and pray that the creatine levels within my baby's little body would stay within normal range. I declare peace over this baby and remove from my life and my family any form of unforgiveness and offense that would bear fruit in the form of sickness within the kidneys, ureter, and bladder. I speak wholeness not only to the forming urinary tract, but I also rebuke any tendency to follow previous generational sin patterns that would open the door to fear, anxiety, or mistrust that would damage those organs later in life.

I decree, precious one, you are a leader! Not because of your personality, but because you will unashamedly follow Christ. Other people will be drawn to you and find their destiny and identity in Christ because of your confidence and leadership.

You will walk in wisdom and discernment beyond your own years and will have the uncanny ability to sense things in your spirit. It will be normal for you to prophecy, through normal conversation, God's promises into the atmosphere and cause even the dead things to come to life. Your faith and trust in God will not be waivered, and though others may fall corrupt with flattery, you will stand and carry out great exploits (Daniel 11:32).

Being Still

Day 1
Read and meditate on the verse below. Who do you think was having this conversation?

Day 2
What could you do to teach your baby that he or she was created in God's image?

Day 3
Which character traits do you have that reflect God? Which ones could stand a little working on?

Day 4

At this point of your pregnancy, your baby can hear and respond to your voice. Let's try an experiment! With your hands cradling your belly, pick the same time each day and speak/pray/sing over your baby. What would you say? I wonder if your baby will respond?

Day 5

Read the verse below. You've been prophetically declaring promises over your baby this trimester. Write a declaration over yourself to use when you feel like you are "not like us."

"Let us make human beings in our image, to be like us."

—Genesis 1:26 NLT

WEEK 32

*"Now the earth was formless and empty, darkness was over
the surface of the deep, and the Spirit of God was hovering
over the waters. . . . Then the Lord God formed a man
from the dust of the ground and breathed into his nostrils
the breath of life, and the man became a living being."*
—*Genesis 1:2; 2:7*

DID YOU KNOW?

✓ Your baby is the size of a squash
seventeen inches long and almost four
pounds.

✓ Your baby is beginning to turn in the
womb in preparation for birth.

✓ The breathing increases from ten to
forty seconds long to help the lungs
produce more surfactant.

✓ All major organs are fully developed.

As my baby begins turning in the womb, I couldn't be more ready to feel those final kicks as my baby makes its way into the birthing position. Lord, I trust your timing and will not allow fear that my baby is not moving into position soon enough to creep into my heart.

Father, you formed man from the dust of the earth, breathed life into him, and he lived (Genesis 2:7). Elijah commanded breath back into the boy, and he lived (1 Kings 17:21–22). Jesus told the disciples "Peace be with you" and then breathed on them, and they received the Holy Spirit (John 20:21–22). So, Father, that same breath that created life, I call on today and say that it will flow freely through my baby's lungs as they are trained, patterned, and regulated this week. My baby will have the ability to produce the necessary surfactant proteins from the adrenal glands and the lungs will become stable after he or she is born.

Abraham, against all hope, believed in hope that the promises you gave him would come to pass and was later rewarded with that promise (Romans 4:18–22). Father, just as Abraham against all hope believed, I put all my hope in you. You are not a man that you should lie (Numbers 23:19), so as I stand on the front line of this next generation and believe that my prayers are being heard in heaven and you will be faithful to your own word.

I decree, my baby, you will be a light in a dark world, and others will sense peace about you and be drawn to you because the Holy Spirit lives inside of you. You will be a deliverer of hope to the nations. Even strangers will seek you out because of the knowledge and wisdom you carry. Your beauty will be great, but the richness and depth of your character is what people will truly seek. You are humble, teachable, and submitted to His voice. You understand intimacy and walk in authority. You are intimately acquainted with His goodness and know the sound of His voice that thunders like a trumpet blast.

Being Still

Day 1

Read 1 Kings 17:21–22. Verse 22, says: 'The Lord heard the voice of Elijah." What do you think was special about his voice that God heard it and answered his prayer?

Day 2

Read John 20:21. Jesus said that just as God sent him, He was sending us. Jesus was given a purpose, and so have we. What is your purpose as it relates to being a mother, a wife?

Day 3

It's easy to understand breath in our physical lives, but what about breathing life into your child to give them spiritual life? What words could you say to them that would give them life in the spiritual realm?

Day 4

How are you feeling this week? Have you noticed that your belly has suddenly popped out? Are you finding it harder to do some of those common things this week that were much easier last week—like tie your shoes?

Day 5

Some women begin getting acid reflux at this time of the pregnancy. Have you noticed this or other symptoms occurring that you've never experienced before?

"This is the message we heard from Jesus and now declare to you: God is light, and there is no darkness in him at all."

—*1 John 1:5*

WEEK 33

"Pray that I may proclaim it clearly, as I should."
—Colossians 4:4

DID YOU KNOW?

✓ Your baby is the size of a head of lettuce, sixteen to seventeen inches long, and is more baby then amniotic fluid.

✓ Your baby is forming more habits like a baby: opening eyes when awake, taking naps, and squinting when sunlight penetrates your belly.

✓ Your baby is developing a stronger immune system to withstand sickness after delivery.

God, I've not stopped believing in divine miracles because I am carrying one right now—inches from my touch. You desire to be known and you seek us relentlessly, yet at times we ignore every sign you show us of your glory and love. This baby in my belly started as a seed planted in my fertile womb and we are a few short weeks from delivery. You are amazing!

Put your hand over my hormones and help my body to effectively use the insulin to prevent gestational diabetes from occurring. Show me how to make time for exercise and become more conscious of the food I eat, so I can decrease the risk of diabetes now and later in life.

God help me through this final stretch! I lift up every white blood cell within my baby's body and speak strength and wholeness as the immune system gets stronger this week. Father, I pray that my baby will never know a day of sickness in his or her life, and that little body will recognize sickness and disease as an attack and rise up to defeat it at its onset. My baby will never be a child susceptible to illness because of the spiritual covering placed over this family.

I decree, my sweet child, you will be a mighty man or woman of God who fears the Lord and understands the authority that you've been granted through the blood of Jesus Christ. You are forming into a beautiful little boy or girl who reacts to the light shown on my belly the same way you will react to the light of God's word when it is read or spoken over your life. You will turn your ear toward it, listen, and respond with passion because you know your Father's voice and walk in his strength and authority given to you by Jesus Christ. You are alert and awake to hear and respond when the Lord calls to you.

Being Still

Day 1

Read Luke 8:40–48. Why do you think the woman was healed of her sickness?

Day 2

How would you compare a person who has no faith to someone who has strong faith? What would be some attributes of each?

Day 3

What would a conversation with someone with strong faith sound like? Jot down a couple of typical sentences you might hear them say.

Day 4

What could be a great way to train your child early to have strong faith in God's promises to us? Think about a couple of very practical things you could do.

Day 5

Creative ideas that instill faith in your children make a huge impression on them. Have you begun thinking of a meal prayer to teach your children?

"She came up behind him and touched the edge of his cloak, and immediately her bleeding stopped.

—Luke 8:44

WEEK 34

*"Listen, my son! Listen, son of my womb! Listen,
my son, the answer to my prayers!"*

—*Proverbs 31:2*

DID YOU KNOW?

✓ Your baby is the size of a five-pound bag of flour and approximately twenty inches long.

✓ You can begin to recognize baby's body parts as your belly fluid decreases.

✓ The intestines, lungs, and central nervous system are continuing to mature.

✓ Your baby's brain is fully developed and is probably dreaming.

✓ Amniotic fluid is one degree warmer than your body temperature.

Father, I call myself blessed because I believed that You would fulfill Your promises to me as I kept my promise to You by caring for my body as well as my baby's (Luke 1:45) during my pregnancy. It was because of a sacrificial love for you and a heartfelt desire that I leave a godly heritage by praying each day over my child. I have decided to draw a line in the sand and choose to believe that my future would be different from my past.

Just as you called Moses to step out into his destiny despite his struggle with stuttering, his murderous past, and his insecurities to fulfill his destiny as a leader (Exodus 3–4), you have called me to be a mother, and I am answering that call and trusting you to teach me how to be a godly one.

As my baby's internal organs and brain continue to develop during these final days and weeks, remove all roots of generational sin tendencies that could cause sickness during development or lead to destructive behavior later in life. Let this child be filled with love, joy, peace, patience, kindness, gentleness, and self-control, and remove right now any root that still remains that could produce strife and conflict—in the Name of Jesus (Galatians 5:22–23).

Darling baby, you will live and not die (Psalm 118:17). You have purpose and destiny; you will do greater things than I've done and will fulfill the purposes God has for you. Little one, you are a leader! The favor of God will be on your life, and you will not back down from adversity.

At a young age, teachers and those in authority will allow you to speak to your peers because of your natural ability to share the promises and the hope that you have in Christ. People will be naturally drawn to you because of the peace you have and the wisdom you carry.

Being Still

Day 1

What areas in your life, even though small, did you ask God to move in and eventually saw an answer come forth?

Day 2

How can you pass that legacy of asking God for help and trusting He will hear you and answer you down to your children?

Day 3

What kind of week are you having thus far? It doesn't have to be anything spiritual or even have anything to do with being pregnant.

Day 4

On week 31 we tried an experiment of cradling your belly at the same time each day and either speaking, singing, or praying over your baby. If you have been doing this, have you noticed your baby responding?

Day 5

Have you begun thinking about what type of delivery you are going to have? Why do you think you selected that?

"I can do all this from Him who gives me strength."

—Philippians 4:13

WEEK 35

"But you are a chosen people, a royal priesthood, a holy nation, God's special possession, that you may declare the praises of him who called you out of darkness into his wonderful light."

—*1 Peter 2:9*

DID YOU KNOW?

✓ Your baby is the size of a spaghetti squash, twenty inches long weighing almost five-and-a-half pounds.

✓ Your baby's shoulders are thickening up in preparation for delivery.

✓ Brain waves are increasing ten times as much as before.

✓ Intestines are filling up with a tar-like waste.

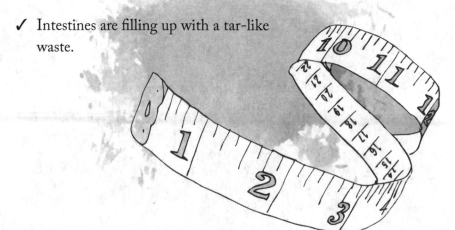

Father, you are a good and faithful father; you have created my baby inside my womb and watched over every detail of development just as you promised in your word (Psalm 139). Lord, I stand in the gap for my baby and declare that good works are ahead (John 17:15–17).

As the brain continues to grow this week, I pray that the four categories of brainwaves (the beta, alpha, theta, and delta) would develop the healthy characteristics needed to function as a normal child.

Father, I pray that my baby will have a mind set on you and follow your path for his or her life and not the ways of the world. Teach them how to renew their mind back to the promises of your word so that no corrupt seed of the world would take root inside them and that this baby would live a life that would lead people back to you (Ephesians 4:23).

Show me how to remain peaceful when I bring correction and speak truth with love and compassion to my baby so that I never break his or her spirit and create other wounds in the process.

I decree little baby, that you are fully surrendered to the Lord, and at an early age you will be a child who eagerly draws near to your heavenly Father and will always be found by Him. You are one who dares to dream big and is not afraid to inquire of the Lord because you understand your position as a son or daughter and know that when you ask, he will do immeasurably more than you can imagine (Ephesians 3:20). Dear one, there is no fear that lives in you, and the words you speak will line up with the promises of God's word. You will not walk with the fear of man, for you are a peace maker and not a peace keeper (James 3:18); you will speak truth to those around you with love and compassion.

Being Still

Day 1
Have you begun more frequent visits to your doctor or health provider? What are they telling you?

Day 2
Has your belly begun to change in form as your body begins to prepare for delivery?

Day 3
Describe what a typical day looks like at this point in your life.

Day 4
Which week would you say you ultimately became fed up with being pregnant?

Day 5
What changes in your daily schedule have been altered or modified because of your growing belly?

"From birth I have relied on you; you brought me forth from my mother's womb. I will ever praise you."

—*Psalm 71:6*

WEEK 36

"As you do not know the path of the wind, or how
the body is formed in a mother's womb, so you cannot
understand the work of God, the Maker of all things."
—*Ecclesiastes 11:5*

DID YOU KNOW?

✓ Your baby is beginning to drop into the
birth canal.

✓ Your baby's ears are sharpening more to
recognize your voice and favorite music.

✓ Your baby's immune system is fully
developed.

✓ Your baby is still relying on your
umbilical cord for food.

Father, in the name of Jesus, I lift up my baby's circulatory and immune system this week. Every nerve ending is intact, and the blood supply is moving through his or her whole body—there will not be any problems supplying all the nutrients to every cell and organ in his body. My baby's immune system is strong, and will be able to fight off every disease, sickness, or illness that would try to attack his or her young body after they are born. The body of this little one is nourished and strong, and I give you all the glory.

Father, my baby has ears that are sharp to hear my voice and recognizes yours when you speak. I have complete trust that you will speak to my baby every day of their life, and they will know in their heart that everything you do is motivated out of love even when those words bring pain and redirection to their plans.

I know you are planning the perfect date for my baby's arrival, and I wait patiently for that date!

I decree my little darling, and I speak peace and order over your life. In the sanctity of my womb where you have lived these last nine months, the Lord has covered and protected you in a quiet place. The Holy Spirit has molded you from the inside out, and just as your body has been growing in the physical, your spirit will begin to flourish and produce fruit that others will glean from. You will be a child who accepts Christ at a young age because you will recognize the presence of the Holy Spirit all around you. My baby, you will hunger and thirst for the word of God and always be a person who watches over the words that come from your mouth because of your love for others to know God as you do.

Being Still

Day 1
As you are getting closer to your due date and hopefully a little more organized, what are you planning on packing for your hospital stay?

Day 2
What are some of the things that you are doing to prepare your home and current family for your newest family member?

Day 3
Has your doctor or healthcare provider given any reason to be concerned with your health and delivery?

Day 4

What will your life look like after delivery? Are you planning on working or staying home full time?

Day 5

What are your thoughts on breast feeding? Have you ever considered making your own baby food?

"This is the message we heard from Jesus and now declare to you: God is light, and there is no darkness in him at all."

—1 John 1:5

WEEK 37

*"See, I am sending an angel ahead of you to guard you along
the way and to bring you to the place I have prepared."*

—*Exodus 23:20*

DID YOU KNOW?

✓ All of the antibodies that you have
developed from vaccinations have been
passed onto your baby to protect him or
her from germs.

✓ At the end of the week, your baby will
be simulating breathing by inhaling and
sucking of the thumb.

Get. this. baby. out. of. me! Ugh—there, I said it! Father, I realize that my baby could come any day now, but even if he or she doesn't, I'll trust your timing! I pray that my baby will remain peaceful at all times and, will always walk in faith in what they cannot see with their natural eyes. I know that my baby will be secure in his or her salvation with your son Jesus at a young age and is destined to be a strong warrior who will always fight forward with your word (Hebrews 4:12).

It seems like all I can do these days is think about what a blessing it will be when I finally give birth to this baby. During these last days, as my body is passing my own antibodies that I've developed through vaccines onto my baby, they will create an immune system to protect them after they're born. I know that my prayers are preparing my baby for spiritual battles that they're now fit to win. Father, I make a prophetic declaration that just like you prepared David in a quiet place for the day he would take on Goliath (1 Samuel 17:45–47), my prayers have gone forth generationally and will be effective, fervent, and righteous (James 5:16) to equip my baby and empower his or her children and grandchildren to withstand the enemy and defeat him. I believe that today, moving forward, my legacy of faith in you will be passed on generationally because of my faithfulness to you.

I decree precious little one, that you will walk into places where others would be affected by the ungodly surroundings yet you will come out unchafed. The Holy Spirit is creating a supernatural "wall" around you that will allow you to be sent into dark places that others dare not go, and you will not be harmed. You will be a person who will be single-minded and focused on the vision and the mission God places on your heart. You will always have a boldness about you that will only be described as "someone who has the hand of God upon them, that God can entrust with a dream to carry out."

Being Still

Day 1

Go to my website www.iamlelis.com and watch this week's video. The video demonstrates how the cervix thins and dilates during labor. Find a balloon and ping pong ball and have some fun! Journal your thoughts!

Day 2

Has your baby kicked and moved more than normal this week? What is the "kicking" inside your heart that you feel God wants you to move forward with?

Day 3

If you have other children, how are they reacting to the new addition soon to be added to their family? What things will need to be different once your baby arrives?

Day 4

Have you begun feeling contractions or Braxton Hicks? Have you had conversations you're your healthcare provider to ensure you will know the difference?

Day 5

Are you beginning to feel the anxiousness of your final count-down to baby delivery? Describe how you're feeling. How have you prepared your home for this next season?

"They trusted in you and were not disappointed.

—Psalm 22:5

WEEK 38

"A woman giving birth to a child has pain because her time has come; but when her baby is born she forgets the anguish because of her joy that a child is born into the world"

—*John 16:21*

DID YOU KNOW?

✓ With your baby swallowing amniotic fluid, some of the first diaper changes will have an odorless, greenish-black, tarry, sticky poop called meconium.

✓ Your baby's lungs are still preparing to expand and contract to prevent air sacs from sticking to the lungs after birth.

Father, just as we are making last-minute preparations in anticipation for the baby's arrival, you are doing the same inside my womb. All week, you have continued to strengthen my baby's lungs, and he or she has been practicing swallowing. You're even adding fat to the brain and nervous system so my baby can react and respond to things outside the protective womb where they've lived these last nine months. You are wonderful, Father—you have not left one thing out, and I am so excited to meet my child. We will wait patiently because you have chosen that perfect date for the blessed arrival, and until that time comes, we will continue to lift him or her up and give you thanks for all that you've done in secret thus far.

Father, I find myself anxious about the upcoming labor and delivery; help me to still my emotions so that my mind doesn't take me places you've never intended it to go. This is one thing I do not have control over and cannot rush. I leave it in your hands.

I decree, my baby that as you draw your first breath and release your voice into the atmosphere, I declare that it will be your first proclamation to the world that you are here, you are in the room, and your voice will be an instrument from God to set the captives free. My baby, I declare that you will be a child who will keep God's word hidden in your heart and discern truth and lies to those hurting around you. Wisdom will fill you in abundance, and others will seek you for the way you share God's truth in love and compassion. Let the words that you speak even as a child, be strong and bold (1 Timothy 4:12), and let your lungs be filled with his breath so when you do speak, the atmosphere will change because you've been saturated with his presence these last nine months.

Being Still

Day 1

What character qualities do you think your baby will have?

Day 2

What legacy did your parents leave for you to follow in?

Day 3

Have you ever wondered about leaving a legacy for your children to follow? What would that look like?

Day 4
What family traditions would you like to begin with your family?

Day 5
If your child could know one thing from you about the last nine months, what would it be?

I love you.

—*God*

WEEK 39

*"You will keep in perfect peace those whose minds
are steadfast, because they trust in you."*

—Isaiah 26:3

DID YOU KNOW?

✓ You have what is officially considered a
full-term baby.

✓ Your baby's body hasn't grown much, but
the brain is still continuing to develop,
even after birth.

✓ Small breast buds are formed on your
baby.

✓ Boys have a tendency to weigh a little
more than girls at birth.

Father, I know you have the exact date prepared for my baby's arrival (Acts 17:26), but I would be lying if I didn't say how anxious I was to see him or her now. Stay close until that day arrives, so my attention is on the amazing gift that is coming and not on whether all the preparations in my home are in order. I am asking you, Holy Spirit, to invade my mind and heart, so I will feel an overwhelming sense of peace and presence as I wait for the appointed time of birth of my son or daughter (Romans 15:13).

Instead of being anxious or allowing myself to be fearful, I will stop, rest my soul, and focus on you. Lord, there are still so many things to do, and thinking about them only magnifies all the things that could go wrong or are still not ready. Can I do this? Am I good enough? There is no turning back now; am I ready, God, really? So I purpose in my heart to know that you have chosen that perfect date for my baby to be born and trust that you are still working inside my womb to strengthen his or her lungs, motor skills, and brain this week so they can adapt to the outside world. I declare that my baby will be a prayer warrior who will take every situation head-on with prayer and thanksgiving and be confident that you will hear them and guard their heart and mind in Christ Jesus.

Peace. Quiet. Stillness. Dear Baby, those are words that describe your spiritual countenance. You will be a child who listens more than you speak. Trusting in the Lord will come easy for you because when the Holy Spirit reveals something in your quiet time, you will take God at His word. Even in times of heaviness and chaos, your unique ability to be still and listen to what the Lord is saying will astound others.

Obedience. Action. Faithfulness. Little baby, those words display your response to the Holy Spirit. You will carry God's presence all the days of your life because being in His presence will never be a chore but water to your soul.

Being Still

Day 1

What is the biggest fear that you have about giving birth? Write that in a life-giving sentence that declares the opposite of your fear and speak it over your life all day.

Day 2

What is the biggest fear that you have will happen in the next few weeks after giving birth? Write that in a life-giving sentence that declares the opposite and speak it over your life all day.

Day 3

What is the biggest fear that you have about yourself? Write that in a life-giving sentence that declares the opposite and speak it over your life all day.

Day 4

What is the biggest fear that you have about your child's life? Write that in a life-giving sentence that declares the opposite and speak it over your life all day.

Day 5

What is the biggest fear that you have about your family's future? Write that in a life-giving sentence that declares the opposite and speak it over our life all day.

"You shall decree a thing and it will be established."

—Job 22:28

WEEK 40

"I waited patiently for the Lord to help me, and
He turned to me and heard my cry."

—*Psalm 40:1*

DID YOU KNOW?

✓ Your baby's skull bones are not
completely fused to assist with delivery
through the birth canal.

✓ Your due date is determined by your last
period, so don't be discouraged if you
think you're late.

✓ Rest assured, it won't be long before
you'll be able to hold your precious baby
in your arms.

Father, my baby knows my voice because they've listened to me sing and pray over them these last nine months. Yet before my baby sees me, he or she first has had an intimate knowledge of you because you sent your Holy Spirit to dwell with them and teach them everything. This baby will know your truth and do even greater things because you have empowered him or her to do so (John 14:12–14).

Just as my baby bonds to hearing my voice at birth, he or she will one day personally recognize your voice again and respond and surrender their life to you. This child will have and enjoy a long life and will always be a child who loves and honors his or her parents (Exodus 20:12).

I pray that my baby would grow into a man or woman who would have a desire to stay close to you and always have a heart that will recognize your voice speaking—even when the world will demand that they give it their attention. I declare that my baby will have a heart of submission to those in authority, and trusting you will always be easy (1 Peter 2:13–17).

Father, you have blessed me with this child, and I will honor and co-labor with you to train him or her in the gifts that you've ordained them even before conception (1 Corinthians 3:9; Romans 8:30). Until that appointed time comes, I sit and wait. I am keeping my heart and emotions still with my eyes only on you.

I decree, child, soon to be born, you will be one who waits patiently on the Lord and never gets disappointed. When the Holy Spirit speaks to you, you will lovingly respond with either waiting or moving forward. Regardless of what you look like on the outside, your spirit man will be "muscular," and you will gain the respect of others around you because of your immovable trust in the Lord's promises.

Being Still

Day 1
Looking back over the last nine months, what were your favorite moments?

Day 2
Which week, month, or trimester of your pregnancy was your favorite and why?

Day 3
What would you say God has taught you during your pregnancy?

Day 4
How has your idea of motherhood, creation, and God's love for you and your child changed during your pregnancy?

Day 5
When your child reads this journal in years to come, what would you like him or her to know?

"I have heard your prayers.

I have seen your tears.

I am healing you."

—*2 Kings 20:5*

REFERENCES

Aranza, Pastor Jacob, Senior Pastor, Our Savior's Church, Lafayette, LA.

Channel Mum | Your Mum Village | An Online Parent Community. https://www.channelmum.com/.

Chopin Amos, Samantha. *My Journey to Wholeness: Was It Physical, Mental or Spiritual?* Xulon Press, Maitland, FL, 2014.

Dr. Seuss. *Horton Hears a Who!* Random House, New York, New York, August 1954.

Kylstra, Chester and Betsy. *Restoring the Foundations: An Integrated Approach to Healing Ministry* (2nd Ed.). Restoring the Foundations Publications, Henderson, NC June 14, 2014.

Leaf, Dr. Caroline. *Switch on Your Brain.* Every Day Baker Books, Grand Rapids, MI, 2015.

MacNutt, Francis and Judith MacNutt, *Praying for Your Unborn Child.* Doubleday, New York, February 2, 1988.

Murkoff, Heidi. *What to Expect When You're Expecting.* Workman Publishing Company, New York, New York, 1984.

Pelton, Kathi. "5779: A Marker Year—God's Goodness Will Be Revealed," Elijah List 9/12/18. www. elijahlist.com.

Styrdome, M. K. *Healing Begins with Sanctification of the Heart: No Disease Is Incurable* (2nd Ed.). https://nuggets4u.files.wordpress.com/2016/01/healing-begins-dr-mk-strydom-2nd-edition.pdf.

Wright, Dr. Henry W. *A More Excellent Way to Be in Health.* Pleasant Valley, February, 2003.

FURTHER HEALING
RESOURCES

The Kitchen Table Counseling & Life Coaching Services
101 Teurlings Drive, Lafayette, LA 70501
www.thekitchentablecounseling.com
337-889-0221

Restoring the Foundations
PO Box 1418, Mount Juliet, TN 37121
www.restoringthefoundations.org
828-696-9075

Be In Health
4178 Crest Highway, Thomaston, GA 30286
www.beinhealth.com
706-646-2074

Christian Healing Ministries
438 W 67 Street, Jacksonville, FL 32208
www.christianhealingmin.org
904-765-3332

SALVATION PRAYER

Dear Lord Jesus, I believe that you're the son of God.
I believe that on the cross you took my sin, my shame and my
guilt and you died for me.

You faced hell for me so I wouldn't have to go.

You rose from the dead and into heaven,
to give me a place in heaven
a purpose on earth
and a relationship with my Father.

Today Lord Jesus, I turn from my sin to be born again.

God is my Father,
Jesus is my Savior,
the *Holy Spirit* is my Helper
and *Heaven* is my home.

In Jesus Name.

Coming Soon—*Sibling Coloring Book*;
Grandparent Prayer Strategy

A PERSONAL LETTER
TO MY CHILD

BEING STILL

_____

_____

_____

_____

_____

_____

_____

_____

_____

_____

_____

_____

_____

_____

_____

_____

_____

_____